The Human Experience

By Mark Porteous

ISBN: 1937055000
ISBN-13: 9781937055004

Dedication

I dedicate this book to my children Alexender and Eden. I believe these revelations will be understood by both of you as the simple truths of life. To *demonstrate* these truths so you can learn, not from my words, but from my actions, is my greatest honor.

Table of Contents

Acknowledgments

My sincere gratitude goes to all of those who have been a part of my journey. My love and thanks go out to my parents; their love and support gave me the foundation to be the man I am today. I have had many parental role models in my life. Not only was I born to the perfect parents for me, but it has also been my good fortune to have stepparents and family friends to offer the guidance I have needed. My sisters, Angie and Marylisa, helped me to better understand and relate with women. Having knowledge and experience in relating to women has been very helpful in creating the beautiful relationship I share with my wife. Renee, you are a wonderful person, an amazing wife, and an incredible mother. You inspire and encourage me. I believe you can do anything. I am honored to be on your team. Together we have created a beautiful family and a magical life. Since childhood, the Dreessen family has shown me that you do not have to be related to be family. My good friends Nikki and Trevor have encouraged me and others to create our own reality. Chris Jasurek clearly demonstrated to me the value of walking the talk. He also shared important editing advice to help me better express my thoughts. Many family members and friends have taught me about love and how to share it. Thank you, Miss Beverly Ford, for shining your brightness and encouraging everyone to shine their own. Thank you, Ashley M. McDonald and Hani for all your excellent editing and advice. I am grateful for the opportunity to experience the divinity of life, the most precious gift we can ever receive. I am happy to be on this great adventure.

Preface

When I was a young boy, my father was an evangelical minister. After my parents divorced, he lost his position with the church. He spent the next several years searching for something in which to believe. He is five years older than my mother. She was sixteen when they married, and she was twenty-eight when they divorced. At the time, she had three children, a strong faith in God, and very little faith in herself. The split left my mom feeling unappreciated and my father in spiritual doubt. These circumstances set the stage for my own personal search. I wanted the appreciation my mother felt she was lacking. I also began my own quest for spiritual truth.

I questioned Christianity. It was the only religion I knew until my teens. I had many questions and doubts. When I was twenty-one, I was introduced to Beverly, owner of The Spiral Circle bookstore in Orlando, Florida. Her presence was peaceful and calming. I felt strangely at home. I knew I was in a good place where people wanted to help others on their own spiritual journey. It was the first time I remember hearing the term *metaphysics*, meaning "beyond the physical." Beverly handed me a book—*The Vision* by Tom Brown Jr. She said she felt that I should read it. I explained that I was just looking. It was my girlfriend who was looking to buy. I was too embarrassed to tell her I did not have money to buy the book. She asked me to take it. If I liked it, I could pay her later. If not, I could bring it back. I was shocked. This was a bookstore, not a library. She did not even know me. How could she afford to take such a risk?

Perhaps she saw something in me that I had not yet seen myself. I had a burning desire for spiritual awakening. She ignited a fire that had been smoldering within me. Not only did I go back to pay for the book, but I purchased *The Quest*, another book by Tom Brown Jr. What I was reading rang true in my core. Ideas I had never been exposed to felt like what I already knew in my heart. Although I had never really enjoyed reading before, I began to read more and more.

Book after book revealed answers to the questions I had been asking since childhood. After meeting Beverly, I began to notice I met just the right people at just the right time to guide me along my chosen path. Now I realize I have something to offer every person who crosses my path, just as they have something to offer me. My thanks go out to everyone who has been a part of my life. Most of all, thank you, Renee, for being my wife.

Part One

Finding Purpose

Chapter One - **Self Discovery**

Ever since man has been aware of his own existence, he has asked, "Why am I here?" Since I was a young child, I have asked the same question. In search of an answer, I have studied many religions, philosophies, and cultures. Some suggest that we are merely toys of a "Supreme Being," being played with like a game of chess. Others say we are here by chance. Many believe we exist in an organized universe, while others believe our universe is chaotic and grows unpredictably. Some live day to day believing the purpose of life is not meant to be known until the body dies. Some just accept a meaningless existence, believing that we are here for a limited time; when the body dies, there is simply nothing left.

Although we have learned what we know from others, we each have the ability to accept or deny the information we receive. No one can convince us of a truth we do not wish to believe. I have chosen to share my thoughts and feelings with you, not to persuade or convince you to adopt my beliefs, but to offer them as possibilities. You might choose to do as I have done with the books I have read—incorporate what *feels* right to you to develop your own spiritual truth.

Do not believe anything because it is said by an authority, or if it is said to come from angels, or from Gods, or from an inspired source. Believe it only if you have explored it in your own heart and mind and body and found it to be true. Work out your own path through diligence.

—Buddha

I do not claim to have original thoughts or ideas about life. Perhaps all truths have already been expressed. Even the great masters, prophets, shamans, and philosophers have shared insights that sound very much the same. Did one teach the rest? Perhaps they expressed similar thoughts because they observed the same truth. There is only one truth. Every individual has a different perspective from which to experience it. As we learn to be more observant, our vantage points improve. I can only speak of my experience and my vision. When I first started to write, I wondered if anyone would care what I think and what made me different from anyone else. After I discovered my purpose in life, I realized I did have something very special to offer anyone looking for happiness.

So, why am I here? Writing this book has helped me answer that question for myself. I don't claim to be a prophet. I am by no means a saint or an angel. I am an ordinary guy with an extraordinary vision. I am offering my own revelations, as I understand them. I see a general purpose that we all share. I am also discovering my own unique purpose. Not only will I propose to you my understanding of the purpose for life on earth, I will tell you how I plan to achieve this purpose.

I have recorded many of the lessons I have learned in the form of poetry. It is a great pleasure to share these thoughts and experiences. First, I would like to offer a view of life from my present perspective. To help with this, I will share a famous quote from Pierre Teilhard-Dechardin:

We are not human beings
Having spiritual experiences.
We are spiritual beings
Having human experiences.

This one passage opened a whole new vista from which to see my life. This expression also inspired me to write the following poem, which, in turn, led to writing this book.

The Human Experience

We have created many vehicles
To transport us from one place to another.
However, there is one vehicle
Greater than any other.

A gift we were each born into,
Each body is as unique
As the spirit that lives inside.
We each experience differently
From the variety of opportunities
Our bodies provide.

A gift received without a warranty,
No one knows how long
They will wear their shell.
But time is not important,
As long as it's worn well.

To make the most of the time we have,
Each in our own way,
Is all that we can do.
Nothing physical will ever see eternity,
This we know is true.

The experiences we share with others,
And even the lessons we learn alone,
Enrich our spirits with wisdom
That, without our bodies,
Never could be known.

Okay, now I have identified what I am—a spirit in a human shell. This does not tell me why I am here. What is the purpose of my human existence?

Finding purpose begins with self-discovery. To discover *why* we are here, first we need to better understand *what* we are. I refer to "we" as both a collective and as each of us as an individual. Collectively, we are a family, a community, a nationality, a race, and a species. Individually, we are composed of three very unique components: body, mind, and spirit.

Our bodies are physical objects made of matter. Matter is anything that has mass and occupies volume. Albert Einstein's Theory of Relativity led to many amazing discoveries, including the relationship of mass and energy. He explained that mass and energy are transmutable. We are familiar with the equation $E= mc^2$. In physics, mass-energy equivalence is the concept that the mass of a body is a measure of its *energy* content. All physical objects are made of energy; therefore, we, our physical bodies, are made of energy. This is a scientific truth.

Because we are self-aware, we realize that we are more than our bodies. Psychology, the study of the mind, was considered to be a branch of philosophy until 1879, when it was developed as an independent scientific discipline in Germany and the United States. The mind is so mysterious it was considered to be philosophical, not scientific. Just as we continue to learn about the physical world, our understanding of the human mind continues to expand. Understanding the power of conscious and subconscious thought is an important part of understanding who or what we are.

Theories can be debated in both physics and psychology. Both subjects are now accepted as science. The controversy gets far more intense when we discuss the theories or even the existence of spirit. If we thought the mind was a mystery, the spirit would seem like magic. How do we scientifically prove the existence of spirit or how it works?

The scientific advancements over the last fifty years have been astonishing. Most of the science we know today has been discovered within the last five hundred years. Before then, we were still able to use the laws of physics, even though we may not have known how or why they worked. Simple tools, like the lever, were used long before Sir Isaac Newton studied the effects of gravitational pull. Perhaps, someday, all human minds will comprehend the human spirit as an integral part of the whole human being. For now, we can look at a simple analogy of scientific method.

There are forces we can detect but cannot see, such as wind. We can look outside a window and know that it is windy. We can see and even hear the effect the wind has on the trees and other objects. Wind itself cannot be seen or heard, Its effect on the environment is what we see and hear. If that example is too elementary, the same thinking is used in science for both the macrocosm of space and the microcosm of quantum physics. Quantum physics is essentially the study of atoms. Studying these tiny particles often requires a different process of observation. Sometimes it is necessary to measure the effects of particles by their interaction with other particles. Also, much of what we know about objects in space is the result of observing their effects on other objects. Planets and black holes have been discovered by the way light reacts with them. One hundred years ago, we could not prove they existed. Just because we cannot prove the spirit exists does not mean it does not. Perhaps someday science will advance to prove the existence of the human spirit. For now, we can have faith that the evidence we see and feel in our lives is assurance enough.

My religion consists of a humble admiration of the illimitable superior spirit who reveals himself in the slight details we are able to perceive with our frail and feeble mind.
—Albert Einstein

Not only is our flesh made of energy, but the human body as a whole is a system of energy known in Eastern philosophy as *chi*. Chi energy plays a major role in our human existence. Everything from our physical health to our emotional well being is related to this energy. The cycle of giving and receiving energy is a part of our everyday life. Sometimes this energy can be expressed as *attention*. When we give attention to someone, we are giving them energy. Depending on the type of attention we are giving, the energy can be positive or negative. Our physical bodies need energy from food, water, and oxygen. Our spirit bodies also need energy. Most people struggle to obtain energy from others. Receiving energy from others is primarily accomplished in two ways: positive attention or negative attention. From childhood, we learn to attract attention by trial and error. When a child learns to use the toilet, he or she is praised. This positive energy feels good. When he or she associates the joy of being praised with the act of using the toilet, the act is reinforced. If he or she is not praised for using the toilet, there is no motivation to do so. If the only attention he receives is disappointment or punishment for not using the toilet, then that energy is what he or she learns to attract. Positive energy is preferred, but in its absence, negative energy is accepted. As long as there is a source of positive energy available, the negative source will be avoided. If the negative energy is all that is available, behavioral patterns are developed to receive this energy instead. As we grow, we find other ways of getting energy. The universe is filled with limitless energy that we can each obtain. By learning to connect with this higher energy, we can become self-sufficient and not compete with others for theirs.

The cover of this book depicts an eye on the side of a pyramid surrounded by an electrically charged sphere. The image represents the three aspects of man: body, mind, and spirit. The gold pyramid is physical and solid. Its structure represents the body, while gold symbolizes material value and worth. Pyramids are considered one of the most durable man-made structures on Earth. It is seven levels high, one for each major chakra. Chakras are energy centers of the body. Chi energy travels through these chakras. Each chakra is associated with its own color and purpose. The seventh chakra is the base or root chakra. Located near the sacrum, it keeps us grounded. It is red. The sixth chakra is the spleen chakra. Located near the naval, it is the power chakra of the lower body—the physical/emotional self. It is orange. The fifth chakra is the solar plexus chakra. Located near the base of the breast bone, it is responsible for human emotion and ego. It is yellow. The fourth chakra is the heart chakra. Located at the heart, it is the love chakra. It is green. Separating the upper and lower body, it brings balance. It is also the threefold flame—love, wisdom, and power. This chakra can be used for healing. The third chakra is the throat chakra. Located near the Adam's apple, it is the communication chakra. It is blue. It is the power chakra for the upper body—the mental/spiritual self. The second chakra is the third-eye chakra. Located in the center of the forehead, it is associated with wisdom. It is indigo or dark purple. The first is the crown chakra. Located at the top of the head, it is our connection to the higher self. It is violet.

The eye represents the mind. It is the door between body and soul. Like the eye, the mind works best when open. In the mind's eye, all thoughts and emotions are created. Our mind, just as our other senses, allows us to observe others and our self. It also controls the body. Imagining our bodies as a vehicle, our mind is the driver. Our mind determines the condition of our bodies and the direction in which we will travel. It is in our mind where all work toward enlightenment or spiritual development begins. Until we understand this concept, no further improvements can be made in body or spirit.

The sphere represents the spirit that powers the body and mind. It is the soul, the higher self. It is pure energy. The soul has made a conscious choice to manifest itself physically in mind and body for the purpose of the human experience. Understanding and developing the connection to our higher self is a vital process in discovering and fulfilling our purpose.

Each of our three parts depends on the other two. It is a symbiotic relationship. When all three forms of self are in tune, each will perform optimally. Self-improvement requires work on all three levels. Our spiritual condition greatly affects our physical existence.

Our physical existence is more than our body and mind. We have all been born into a number of unique conditions. Each variation creates different opportunities from which to experience. Geography alone has a great effect on perspective. Geography can influence climate, nationality, religion, wealth, and health. All can play a role in our development. Individual characteristics such as race, gender, and family have more specific effects. Time can also play a role. We can have different experiences now than we could have one hundred years ago. Even a decade can make a difference. Who is to say one day could not make a difference? Each additional variable adds exponential possibilities of perception. Race and gender can offer very different opportunities, even more so in some nationalities and religions. Nothing influences our development more than the family into which we are born. Our families are a reflection of their families and society. Culture shapes our earthly being.

As our hierarchy of human needs is fulfilled, we develop self-awareness and the ability to choose *who* we are. *What* I am is a body, mind, and soul. *Who* I am is reflective of the choices that I make. Life is full of choices. We choose what we make out of life. We can choose happiness. Instead of finding blame or excuses for our situation, we can look for the best response to better ourselves. Accepting and understanding this concept is crucial before moving on with our growth as a person. This is where our quest begins.

Chapter Two - **The Quest**

Embarking on the quest toward enlightenment is a conscious choice. The path is riddled with obstacles. Changing obstacles into opportunities is a matter of perspective. Our perception creates our reality. Greater perspective is one reward for choosing to elevate our existence. As we elevate ourselves and gain perspective, we are better able to create opportunity from obstacles. Our reality becomes an escalating spiral circle of ever-improving circumstances. This cycle begins with a choice.

Once we choose this journey, it makes sense to take inventory of our available resources to assist us. Sailors have always relied on many tools for a successful voyage. Engineering vessels is an ancient craft. Long before physics was understood, heavy ships were built to stay afloat in treacherous waters. Sails and oars were used for propulsion. The sails harnessed the wind, a powerful force of nature, to move them. Rudders were designed to control direction. Many instruments were developed to guide them. They would navigate using sextants to determine their coordinates from celestial bodies. They used the stars themselves as mile markers. They had almanacs and maps recorded from previous travels. They had ships full of men they counted on for support. They learned from experience to follow their own instincts.

Tools of the Quest

We are provided all the tools we need to become self-actualized for the voyage of life. Free will, the power of choice, engages the law of attraction to draw that which we create in our mind and our higher consciousness into our lives. People come into our lives to guide us and support us through different legs of our trip. Synchronicities open doors to new revelations. We were all born with instincts to protect us. Intuition is not learned; it is our natural connection to the world around us. As we develop our physical senses, we lose our connection to this powerful gift. The Source connects us to all things and fulfills all our needs. The laws of the universe apply to all, even those who do not believe. We do not need to believe the earth is a sphere to sail around it. We do not need to believe in gravity for it to pull on us. If we chose to believe what we have learned from our own experience and trust what we have seen and felt, we can better utilize the universal laws as tools of greater learning. Mastering the use of these tools enriches our experience and accelerates our trek.

Free Will: Steering/Direction

Free will is the spiritual force that grants each of us the responsibility to create our own future. Our own free will is the **only** control we have in life. Once we recognize the karmic effects of our thoughts, words, and actions, we become more conscious, our intuition becomes more heightened, synchronicities become a consistent guide to keep us on track, and we open our connection to All That Is, The Source, God, or whatever name you prefer to use. God is Love. Love is our most powerful gift. No matter what happens in life, we choose how we will allow it to affect us.

I Am the Captain

I am the captain of my own ship.
Let the winds blow where they may.
I can't change the wind.
I can't escape the storms.
I will take what I get
And make the most of it.

My life is a ship on the open seas.
I may run my ship any way I please.
I choose the place where I'd like to be.
The course I set is up to me.

Placing my faith in the hands of four winds,
I bare my soul and face my sins
In any direction they may blow.
Still, I decide where my ship will go.

If for some reason off that course I am thrown,
A new corrective course I must set on my own.
Waves and tides will always be. These I cannot arrange.
I accept and appreciate all I cannot change

The wind and the storms are beyond my control.
They weathor my ship and strengthen my soul.
Caught in storms, winds may not be with me.
Through darkness, stars I may not see.

Winds may blow my battered ship astray.
In the end, I always know I will be okay.
Skies will clear. Storms will pass.
Sea and wind will calm at last.

Should my ship be taken
By the treacherous sea,
I've done all that I can do.
It was simply meant to be.

If my quest was not intended,
The mighty seas I know will end it.
For every day that I survive,
I thank God to be alive.

I am truly grateful
For all that I have seen.
I will continue sailing
And heading toward my dream.

The decisions of my life
Are still left for me.
As captain of my ship,
I steer my destiny.

When we plan a trip to an unfamiliar destination, how do we choose which route to take? Do we ask only our most traveled friend and follow his suggestions? Or do we compare several alternate routes to see which one best suits our needs? Some individuals prefer the speed or ease of expressways, while others prefer the beauty and diversity of back roads. Each offers different possibilities. Ultimately, we must choose the route most likely to offer what we feel will benefit us most. This is a personal choice. Just as we have the right to choose our own path, it is important to allow others to choose their own without judgment. So, now I must plot my own course. But how will I know if I am on track? Are there any tools or instruments to tell me whether or not I am going in the right direction? How do I gauge my progress?

Relationships: Compass/GPS

From the moment of conception, we each have been given the most intricate and precise tool to know who we are and where we are going—relationships. Relationships serve as both a mirror to see *who* we are and a GPS (global positioning satellite) to find our bearings and know *where* we are in our progress. To know what kind of person you are, look at the people with whom you spend the most time. Do they inspire you or irritate you? The qualities in others that inspire us are the qualities within that thirst for nourishment. Traits that bother us most are usually the ones we most need to address internally. For parents, the most accurate measurement of where we are is our children. What qualities do you appreciate the most in your children? Where do you think they got them? What behaviors would you most like them to change? Where did they learn them? Can you see the similarities between the personalities of your children and your own? Identifying similarities in the people close to us is the best way to work on personal development.

It is our relationship with family, friends, lovers, and strangers that sculpt us into who we are. Being consciously aware of our relationships, on a spiritual level, enables us to learn to use this tool to its highest capacity. The first relationship we form is naturally with our parents, specifically our mother. That bond begins immediately after birth. Our parental bond creates the foundation for how we will build relationships for the rest of our lives. I believe we are born into the families that were intended for us. This does not mean a child of an abusive or neglectful parent deserves to be mistreated. I am simply suggesting that Universal Wisdom knows what an individual can handle and that great strength can come from very difficult experiences. We must play the cards we are dealt. What seems like the best hand does not always win. Many individuals develop strong character from challenging situations, while others make little use of abundance and prosperity. We learn from our parents how to behave. Not only do we learn by mimicking parental behavior, we also develop our personalities as a reaction to the way we are raised. Whether we are strong and confident or timid and fearful is a reaction to our upbringing. Once we are aware of how our parents affected our development, we can choose to embrace our strengths and overcome our weaknesses. As we mature, the relationships we form begin to more clearly reflect who we have chosen to be. If we seem to be surrounded by negative people, we can identify negativity within ourselves. When we address our own issues, the external negativity will tend to drift away or lose its effect on us.

Relationships will continue to shape who we are, whether we are aware of their effects or not. By understanding our relationships, we can better understand ourselves. The universal law of attraction causes us to draw people into our lives who can teach us what we most need to know about ourselves. Our relationships directly reflect who we are. This is more apparent in intimate relationships. An intimate relationship can be like being under a microscope. We can see each other's personality in minute detail. We also see what types of people we attract and to whom we are attracted. This also tells us a lot about ourselves. Although less apparent, this reflection of self is also true in relationships we may not consciously choose. The way we relate to our coworkers, friends of friends, in-laws, and even family is a direct reflection of who we are in that moment. Unaware that we are looking in a mirror, it is easy to see in others the traits that need correction within ourselves. Even the way we treat ourselves tells of who we are. In most cases, we react toward ourselves in relatively the same manner as we would toward another person. Every relationship is a model for the experiencing of one's self. Experiencing one's self is an important process in learning how to fulfill our purpose and is a valuable benefit in relationships. Another vital lesson we learn from others is unity. Finding similarities in others rather than focusing on the differences creates common bonds. Working together, we are able to accomplish far more than we can individually. Seeing all beings as part of the same collective whole, we can work toward a civilization of oneness instead of separation. Unity breeds compassion and tolerance.

We have three types of relationships: our relationship to others, our relationship to ourselves, and our relationship to God. No *one* of these relationships is complete by itself. To be completely fulfilled, each of these types of relationships is dependent on the other two. As we mature and develop, each of these relationships increases through our capacity to love. Like a marriage, each entity is one with the other. Seeing ourselves as part of the whole and not as isolated, helps us to see others the same way. This develops a sense of unity instead of separation. Although each relationship is developed simultaneously, each is essential in developing a healthy relationship with God. Being one with The Source is a crucial precedent in developing other relationships. Understanding that we are a part of God and that God is in every one of us means that we are each divine creations. We have importance and value. We are co-creators. We have a purpose in this life and deserve to be loved. Self-worth is important for developing a relationship with one's self, and we can only love ourselves as much as we truly love others. I like to use the airplane emergency analogy. At the beginning of every commercial flight, the flight attendants explain the emergency procedures. In case of emergency, oxygen masks will drop from the overhead compartments. They say to put on your own mask before assisting your children. The reason for this is so you do not pass out due to lack of oxygen. If your children pass out while you are putting on your mask, you can still help them and they will be okay. If you pass out, they may not be able to help you. It is important to take care of yourself so that you can be in the best position to help others. After developing our relationship to ourselves, we can better relate to others. By learning with and loving others, we enrich our relationship and love toward All That Is. Learning to master our human relationship to self and others enables us to fulfill our purpose of being born into this human experience.

I was often told that there are different kinds of love. We love our family one way, our friends another, our spouse another, and the stranger on the street yet another way. We are supposed to love everyone—but love everyone differently. I believe a better goal would be to love everyone the same, but relate to each person differently. To do this, we first have to understand what love is. The word love is so overused that its definition has become vague and distorted. By referring to our passion for material goods as love, we diminish the value of the word *love*. As much as one may enjoy certain foods, activities, or objects, we cannot love these things. Psychology defines love as unconditional, positive regard. Do we love food if it is spoiled, a car that doesn't run, or a game we don't understand? We can love a person, but can we love *unconditionally*? As long as we truly love ourselves, it is possible to love even the most flawed individual without allowing his or her flaws to burden us. I believe there is one kind of love we can share with everyone, including ourselves. Although we relate to different individuals on different levels, we can love all people. I believe there are several main virtues necessary in the development of total love. Without exercising all of these virtues, one cannot truly demonstrate unconditional love. With these virtues, we can learn to enjoy more satisfying relationships of all types—with family, friends, acquaintances, lovers, ourselves, and even with God. These principles are necessary to fulfill our purpose on earth. Love is a powerful tool we are each given from the Creator. We are offered an endless supply. Regardless of the love we have received from others, we all have the capacity to give love. Our capacity to give is limited only by our connection to The Source. We can tap directly into The Source anytime we choose. We are one with the Source.

Religion: Maps to Enlightenment

I remember times when I felt alone and detached from The Source. As so many do when they see no other choice, I searched for a connection through religion. Early in my quest for spiritual truth, I came to the conclusion that religion is man's feeble attempt to explain what we believe but do not understand. I found religion to be weighed down by dogma and politics. Well-meaning, enlightened individuals who wished to help humankind started most religions. Over time, religion has become a political tool to control the masses. Many of the original messages have been lost or convoluted. Many religions, including the two largest religions, Christianity and Islam, have split into multiple factions. These two groups have more similarities than differences, yet they somehow tend to find conflict with each other and even within their own groups. Most individual practitioners follow their chosen religion for personal growth. Others follow out of fear or guilt. With a positive *intent*, a person can improve by following any cultivation practice. Most teach the same important lessons. If practiced, not just studied or preached to others, we can grow spiritually on whichever path we choose.

If my destination is to be with God (which is really everyone's destiny), I can get there by any route I wish to take. I can take the long way and enjoy the scenery or the expressway and arrive more quickly, depending on my needs or desires. Contrary to the belief of many, no one religion or philosophy holds the one and only way. *God is too big for one religion.* Although no one religion is able to summarize or own God, all major religions offer a path toward enlightenment. Abraham, Jesus, Muhammad, Krishna, Buddha, and Lao Tzu were history's greatest teachers. The evidence is the endurance and growth of the mutated religions that were based on their teachings. They shared many common lessons. The most important of all was that anyone can find Nirvana. We can each live in heaven on earth right now. We have to get there ourselves. They did not walk the path for us. They showed us the way that worked for them and offered guidance. Before Jesus' early followers were called Christians, they were called "Followers of the Way." In *Toa Te Ching*, Lao Tzu taught the "Great Way." Buddha followed the "Middle Way." There are many parallels. They all emphasize the personal journey *within*. We can choose to follow any path we wish.

Knowing that I am indeed a spirit in a human shell and that I have free will to go in any direction I wish, where do I go from here? What is my ultimate destination? I want to elevate myself. I want to be closer to God, whatever God may be. All That Is, The Universal Power—the name we give it is irrelevant. This is not a religious concept. It is philosophical. I want to be as close to The Source as I can while still in my human shell. How do I get there? So many religions and philosophies offer different routes. Many contradict each other. Which path should I take?

Detours

When cruising down life's highway,
No matter where you want to go,
There are many routes to get there;
Some you may not know.

In choosing a path to follow,
Many factors will help you to decide,
Whether you are in a hurry
Or just going for the ride.

Many maps will be shown to you
Of different routes to choose.
Once on the road, you must decide
Which ones you will use.

Plot your course ahead of time,
But do not fear a change of mind.
Maps are simply guides
Of routes others have chosen to find.

Much of life's greatest scenery
Is off the beaten path.
Often, roads are missed
When driven by too fast.

The path to your destiny,
Just perhaps,
May be on a detour
And not on any maps.

A spiritual quest is a personal journey. Religion can be a helpful guide to navigate our way. It can be dangerous, too. Many offer different types of guidance, but there are more similarities than differences between 90 percent of the religions. Focusing on commonalities encourages unity. I have found it useful to have some understanding of all the major religions of the world. Understanding the history of religions and how they relate to each other is interesting and an important process in seeing the bigger picture. Practicing one path exclusively can offer a great degree of detailed knowledge and wisdom but limits one's self to a single perspective. Knowing the basics about several paths offers a broader understanding of man's interpretation of God and the laws of the universe. Finding the similarities between different religions is the only way to bring peace to the world or inner peace to ourselves. Sharing philosophy and beliefs is a wonderful opportunity for everyone to see different perspectives. We all come from the same place, yet we each have different views.

Religion is sometimes considered synonymous with spirituality. I see religion as *structure* and spirituality as *content*. Although religion is intended as a road map to a successful spiritual life, many religions reinforce the concept of separation between us and God. Promoting themselves as the only conduit to God, religions self-propagate the need for their existence. Much like the human ego, the first priority for many religions seems to be self-preservation, and with it comes the incessant need to be "right." For one to be right, one must feel that *others must be wrong*. Deep rifts continue to grow even among different sects within the same religion. Ritual and tradition have value but can distract from the purpose. Adherents are often so devout, they get caught up on the words, which lose their overall meaning. Tolerance is often forgotten between individuals with conflicting religious beliefs. Guilt and fear prevent followers from questioning authority or searching elsewhere for truth. Once we learn to develop a personal direct connection to The Source, we free ourselves to be led by God rather than someone else's interpretation of what God wants for us.

By limiting mortal access to God only through the church, the church is given the ultimate power. Religion, by its organizational structure, becomes political. It becomes a tool to control the masses. The structure begins with the best intent, as organization can be a good alternative to chaos. Enlightened ones share their insights as rules or laws of the universe. These laws are meant to inspire and encourage people to develop a direct connection to The Source. However, what they have become seems very different. Being raised a Christian, it was subconsciously ingrained in me that the only way to have a relationship with God was through Jesus. In John 14:6, Jesus said to him, "I am the way, and the truth, and the life. No one comes to the Father except through me." This verse is taught to mean that we can only have God in our lives, or be with Him in the afterlife, by believing Jesus died for our sins. Based on the way Jesus lived, it has always seemed to me he meant the only way to live a life with God is to be *like* Him, to follow His example.

I had so many conflicting feelings between Christianity, the religion I was first taught, and what I believed about my own spirituality. I knew there were many other spiritual beliefs. I decided to learn the basic fundamentals of all the major religions of the world. Understanding world religion explains a lot about modern society. Religion began as man's interpretation of what he believed God to be. It was an attempt to understand our own spirituality and our relationship to All That Is. Religion is man-made rules, spirituality is innate, philosophy is intellectual opinion.

Nearly 80 percent of the world's population identifies with one of four religions. Christianity is the dominant religion, with 33 percent; second is Islam, with 21 percent; and Hindu is third, with 14 percent. Buddhism and Chinese traditional religions (Taoism and Confucianism) combined account for 16 percent. Just over 8 percent consider themselves spiritual but not religious. Another 8 percent are agnostic ("one who is not committed to believing in the existence or non-existence of God") or atheist. All the rest of the religions combined, including Judaism, make up less than 6 percent of the world's population. The number of adherents does not make one religion more valid than another. One-third of the world is communist. That does not make it the best form of government.

About 75 percent of Americans consider themselves to be Christian. When I was a child, my father was a minister of an Evangelical church. Several ideas bothered me. The major one was how God could punish people who live highly moral and spiritual lives but have not heard of Jesus or simply have different beliefs, while another person who lives an immoral life void of compassion is rewarded for believing that Jesus died to forgive all of his or her sins. I saw a lot of hypocrites in church. Many would sin Monday through Saturday, be forgiven on Sunday, and then start the cycle over again. I did not see how these people would live for eternity in heaven, while a highly spiritual Buddhist monk who lived a life of truth, tolerance, and compassion would spend eternity in hell. No person knows for sure what happens after we die. Instead of living my life for what may or may not happen after I die, I have chosen to live each day as a gift of God.

In my pursuit for spiritual development, I have enjoyed experiencing different cultivation practices. One practice I studied along my journey was Falun Gong. It is based on the Buddhist belief system. I learned many lessons while studying this cultivation practice: I learned from what I did not like about it, as well as what I did like. What impressed me most were the things that bothered me about other religions: the method of "spreading the word," the focus on tithing, and the need to control individuals and the masses through fear and politics. Falun Gong does not collect money or ask for tithing or donations. More importantly, practitioners do not try to convert others. They do not send out missionaries to "witness." They do not fight wars in the name of God. Like Tai Chi, they meet in public and allow others to join and ask questions if they choose. Also, they do not condemn those who do not believe as they do. They do not use fear tactics or politics to control people's behavior. They promote practicing in any environment. One does not need to change his line of work or location to become involved. In fact, they encourage involvement without making changes in your career, unless it is counterproductive to spiritual growth. It may be easier to walk the spiritual path living in a temple, yet we can often learn more of life's lessons from living an ordinary, daily life. I have reminded myself of this point many times. I find it very rewarding and encouraging learning how to apply my spiritual beliefs in a world that believes so differently from what I am familiar with. It is important to learn how to apply the principles in everyday life, in ordinary situations. It is everyday life that offers the greatest experiences from which to learn. This realization helped me begin to discover my own personal purpose.

The biggest issue I have with Falun Gong is the belief in "one path." Although Falun Gong teaches that many paths can lead us to enlightenment, practitioners believe we must chose one system and follow that system *only*. They disapprove of my "chicken soup method" of taking the ingredients I like from many recipes. This opinion is very difficult for me to reconcile. I believe just the opposite. I have always said my God is too big to fit into any *one* religion. To me, religion is man trying to create a box in which to fit God. No one truly knows the whole universal truth. No debate can prove a theory more accurate than any other. We are born knowing right from wrong. From birth, we are programmed how to believe. The light inside each of us connects us to the truth. Spirituality is innate; religion is external dogma. The words that fill this book are ingredients I have borrowed from others to create my own recipes. They are appetizing to me. Take from them what you chose. I hope you find much to enjoy.

The Law of Attraction: Propulsion

The Law of Attraction has become a common term since I first started my journey. Many great books, such as *The Secret*, have been written about just this one subject. It is a very simple and very powerful universal law. What we send out will come back. We reap what we sow. Our thoughts, words, and actions send messages out to the universe. The messages we send out return to us in the form of manifestations. We program our own future. If we focus on what we feel we are lacking, we will continue to lack those things. If we appreciate all we have received, we will continue to receive.

People have often told me I am very lucky. It used to offend me that they thought my life was so good because of many random occurrences. Instead, I liked to say I was blessed. Not that I was any better than anyone else or that God liked me more. I had good fortune because I was practicing *The Secret* before I had ever heard of it. Once I understood how it worked, I tried even harder to be conscious of the messages I was sending out to the universe. Simple rules we are taught as children can have a huge impact on our lives. My mom used to tell me, "If you do not have anything nice to say, then don't say anything at all." Now I not only censor my words, but I control my thoughts, too. When negative thoughts come into my mind, I first ask myself where it is coming from. Then I find a way to replace it with a positive thought. For instance, if I am driving and get cut off by another driver, I often get angry. If so, I ask myself why I am feeling that way. The answer is I am angry because the other driver is being reckless and endangering my life and that of others. I then take a deep breath and feel grateful that I am no longer the foolish driver I used to be. I am grateful that the driver's foolishness did not cause me any harm. Such an event brings my consciousness into the present moment. Instead of thinking about where I am going or what else I need to do for the day, I become more aware of the drivers around me and my own driving. This makes me thankful for being in the moment. It reminds me how wonderful my life is and all I have for which to be thankful. A minor event that evoked anger became a reminder of my blessings.

Luck is more about perception than experience. Every day we drive to work but never say, "Wow, I made it. I feel lucky." If we were pulled from a car after a bad accident, we might pause to think, "My car is totaled, but I feel lucky to be alive." Finding fortune in a bad situation is a key element to blissful living. If we can learn or grow from what seems to be a bad experience, the good experiences are valued as even greater blessings. Appreciating even the smallest blessings as good fortune makes the big blessings more meaningful. A person may appear to have everything he could want, but if he does not appreciate it, he may still feel unlucky. Others may seem to have nothing and feel blessed with what they do have. We have all been blessed with the gift of life. Most of us are in the top 10 percent of the wealthiest people on the planet. Yet, one might feel unlucky because he or she still has not won the lottery and must work to pay his or her bills, while a homeless person feels lucky for a dollar he just received.

To be lucky, we have to feel lucky. We do that by appreciating all we have. This sends a message to the universe that we are lucky. The universe then responds by manifesting good fortune in our life. It is important to be conscious of the good fortune as it comes. Acknowledging our blessings makes us feel lucky, and the message continues to go out to the universe. Another way to increase good luck is to find good fortune in misfortune. After surviving an accident or an illness, feeling blessed to be alive instead of focusing on the negative is rewarded with more blessings. Some people see themselves as always getting bad luck. The universe hears their message and continues to give them challenges to complain about.

I believe we create our own luck. Thomas Jefferson wrote, "I'm a great believer in luck and I find the harder I work, the more I have of it." Luck is not a coincidence. It is a combination of what we send out to the universe and how we perceive the manifestations that we receive. A friend posted a story about her three-year-old daughter on Facebook. She had worked tirelessly on a fundraiser for a club she was in, and my friend explained to her daughter that because she had worked so hard and done such a good job she could choose how she wanted to spend her share of the money. Her daughter thought for only a moment before telling her mom, "I already have so much. Why don't we give it to someone who isn't as fortunate?" That is a lucky girl. Her mom taught her to appreciate all she has. In doing so, she will never feel a lack for anything. The extra bonus of learning about charity will surely enrich that little girl's life and those around her.

Intuition: Divine Voice

Intuition is a special power we have all been given. It is our higher self speaking to our conscious minds. It is our Divine Voice. This voice is often underestimated. We all have intuition. It seems like some people are better able to hear their inner voice. Actually, it is not about being able to hear; it is being able to listen. We hear words every day that go in one ear and out the other. We learn to shut out so much noise in our lives. Like a spam filter on a computer, our minds filter the information we choose to absorb. Sometimes, if we filter out too much, we can miss important messages. By paying attention to details and being alert, we become aware of signs all around us. Our higher self is naturally able to decipher the messages we get. How our conscious minds react to information perceived by our higher consciousness affects how the flow of information will continue. If we stop listening, eventually we stop hearing. We learned early in our relationship that my wife, Renee, has very strong intuition—and that it is worth paying attention to it. As we started paying more attention, the messages have become louder and clearer. Intuition is instinctual. It is our most primal survival tool and a powerful resource.

Imagination: Creative Source

Imagination is the key to creativity. It is the source of our innovation. All man-made creations begin in the imagination. We also use our imagination to create solutions to problems we face. The dictionary offers three definitions for imagination: 1) The faculty or action of forming new ideas, images, or concepts of external objects not present to the senses, 2) The ability of the mind to be creative or resourceful, 3) The part of the mind that imagines things. We are taught to encourage children to use their imaginations, yet somehow, many of us seem to forget the joy of using ours as we get older. The expression of our imagination through art, music, writing, and other outlets allows our mind to focus on creating, which distracts us from the mundane thoughts of everyday life. It is through imagination that we evolve individually and together as a species.

Love: Universal Energy

Ultimately, the quest toward enlightenment is an inward journey requiring deep soul-searching. I have found meditation to be one of the greatest vehicles assisting in the search. Meditation allows us to dig into our own minds to reunite our own direct connection to The Source through our higher self. There are many ways to meditate. Various techniques can be used, and it does not have to be complicated. Just giving yourself five minutes of silence every day will encourage you to find ways to get more. Find a place where you can create a calm, quiet sanctuary. It can be done almost anywhere. I have reached incredible heights while meditating in a closet. I have parked my car at convenience stores and in parking lots. After turning off the music and my cell phone, I close my eyes and take a deep breath. Allowing my mind to wander freely with all the thoughts of the day before releasing them can be a nice way to clear the mind. Whether you choose a thought or word on which to focus; a speck of light; or light that surrounds you entirely, a focal point can quiet the mind from its many distractions. Once we can achieve a quiet, conscious mind, we will be able to hear the voice of our own higher consciousness. This is the most important matter I can impress upon people. It is our own direct connection to The Source that will best guide us. I cannot overemphasize the importance of listening to your inner voice, your Divine Voice. To hear it, people must shut out the noise in their heads. That noise has been created by the conscious mind in an attempt to address external fears. One day while meditating, I had the following conversation with my higher self:

I asked my higher-self, what is our purpose for being incarnated?

The general purpose of life on earth is to learn how to love completely so that we may reflect the glory of God. This purpose is achieved through our relationship to self, others, and God. This might seem unrealistic and idealistic to some. It is a lofty goal, but it is not out of reach. This is why we are here, not merely to love, but to be love, to represent God in a physical, mental, and spiritual form.

We are Human. How can we *be* love?

Jesus was love. He transcended above living a merely physical existence while still within his human body.

That was Jesus, the Son of God. I am mortal. It is blasphemy to say I could be what Jesus was.

Are we not all the children of God? Jesus did not want us to worship him. He wanted us to be like him. He did not do all our work for us. That would rob us of our own purpose. He simply led the way. It is up to us to follow. He showed us that we can be one with God while being humans on this earth. There have been many examples of humans who have chosen to become enlightened and represent God while still on this earth. We are all more than just physical bodies. We are body, mind, and spirit. We are all God's creation. Just as art is an expression of man, man is an expression of God.

I learned that I am here to have a relationship with God. As I am a part of The Whole, it too is a part of me. I can *be* love only through that relationship. We are all mirrors of God's greatness. We all reflect the glory of God. After all, God is All That Is. Referring to God as *Him* is personification. It helps us to identify. He is what we call "good." He is also what might be labeled "evil." He is all-encompassing. There is nothing outside or separate from Him. Only in our own minds can we separate ourselves from God. Rather than viewing God as a being, I see God as the sum total of all that is; therefore, there is no "good" or "bad." In terms of a sea voyage, God is the wind, the sea, the boat, the crew, the stars, and the storms. God is timeless and without form. What we see as the known universe is enormous, yet it is still a small fraction of all that God is. My journey is not to understand God, but to return to the oneness with God that is our natural state. It is a state of love. The Source is love.

Part Two

Virtues of Love

The process of developing an intimate relationship with God is life's challenge and life's reward. This is how we learn to *be* love. This is why we are here. This is not a process that occurs overnight. It is a goal to work toward. Each of us can choose to work toward this goal at our own pace or we can choose to ignore it altogether. It is our choice. If you feel any desire to grow in this direction, I believe the following pages will be helpful and will explain my understanding of the virtues necessary to build human relationships founded in true, complete love. Although I have a long way to go, it is my goal to master these virtues. By *practicing* the knowledge I am now sharing with you, I aim to grow personally and maximize my own existence and also be an example of how we can all evolve toward the same goal. It is through our human relationships that we learn the skills necessary to build a real relationship with God. These skills or virtues that I am about to discuss are not new. They are taught in many cultures, religions, and philosophies. What I am offering is my understanding of and experience with these important skills.

Some religions speak of the seven deadly sins and their corresponding virtues. I practice three virtues: tolerance, compassion, and truth. I believe these three virtues and their corresponding subsets encompass the full meaning of love. Truth is the pinnacle. *Trust* and *honesty* are vital in any healthy relationship. It is our choice to use them. Truth is much bigger than just our relation to others. With our human eyes, we cannot see truth completely. We see all things with prejudice of our human perspective. Not even from the tallest mountain can the whole world be seen. Truth is *omniscient.* With the limitations of the human perspective, it would be easy for us to say we are only responsible for the truth we know. It must be our own choice to listen to what we know is right inside, not what has been taught to us from others. Compassion is *appreciation* and *respect.* With appreciation and respect comes charity. Compassion is giving. It is an expression from within, a connection with The Source. It is the Buddha nature. Tolerance is *forbearance* and *fortitude.* Three great strengths—*faith, acceptance,* and *forgiveness*—build tolerance. Faith is a belief in truth. Faith is a choice. With or without faith, truth will continue to exist.

Our pilgrimage is a great road to travel alone; it's even better with company. We find many unexpected faces frequently crossing our increasingly busy path. A critical mass is forming. More people are beginning to understand how these simple tools can guide us toward joy and happiness through a direct personal connection to God. Regardless of religious or political alignment, people are coming together to raise the group consciousness of the human race. Decades ago, a spiritual renaissance began. We are participating in the human experience during a time when the masses are seeing the opportunity to self-actualize. Love is the way. Practicing these virtues on a highly conscious level in ordinary situations provides the experience needed to grow spiritually. These principals can guide us in any situation we might face in any aspect of our lives—personal, work, or family. Truth, compassion, and tolerance express love in any experience.

Chapter Three - **Tolerance**

Tolerance implies no lack of commitment to one's own beliefs.
Rather it condemns the oppression or persecution of others.
—John Fitzgerald Kennedy

Tolerance is the foundation for spiritual growth. I am referring to both forbearance, the capacity to endure pain or hardship, and the act of allowing without judgment. How we relate to others and handle difficult situations offers us opportunities to practice tolerance. Having the fortitude to withstand suffering and accepting people with different beliefs than our own are integral parts of spiritual evolution. *Faith* makes us strong. *Acceptance* makes us pliable. *Forgiveness* propels us and keeps us moving forward. Having *faith*, being able to *accept*, and being able to *forgive* all contribute to our strength of tolerance.

Faith – Knowing something to be true without scientific proof. Faith is internal and often contradicts tangible evidence.

There are different kinds of faith. Superficial faith is our belief in a specific result. Whether that faith is in ourselves or others, we can feel let down when our desired result is not achieved. Deeper faith is belief in the overall outcome, regardless of the situation. It is belief in the unknown. What we desire is not always what is best for us. No matter how the result may appear, in faith we know all things happen for the greater good. When we place our faith in a person, we believe they will succeed, despite their shortcomings. Success is relevant. What may seem to some as failure can be turned into future success. Faith is given freely. Trust is earned. We pay for trust with honesty. Faith rewards us with strength and courage.

To Live Without Faith

I looked into the future
And feared that I was lost.
I tried to believe
That I would make it through okay
By searching for hidden answers
And that faith would lead the way.

The harder I searched to find a path to follow,
The more I feared there was no way out.
My faith was pushed to the very edge.
That's when The Voice began to shout,

"Your faith is empty.
It will lead you nowhere.
It will leave you dying in this wretched place."
That was all it took
To see my fear and look it in the face.

Then I responded back,
I would rather die in faith
Than to live without it.
I'll stand and face my fears.
And so I did...
As I watched them disappear.

In a religious context, faith usually refers to something outside of ourselves, something bigger than we are. Instead of separating ourselves from this greatness, I prefer to believe *I am part* of something much greater than our human minds can comprehend. Faith is the cornerstone of all virtues. When I speak of faith, I do not mean following blindly. It is an internal awareness, a knowing. It is belief in a higher consciousness. This knowing allows us to exercise acceptance.

Acceptance – Allowing "what is" to be in the here and now without resistance.

Learning to accept whatever life may throw at us is not easy. It takes constant practice. Acceptance sounds so passive. It can conjure up an image of weakness, when, in actuality, it is a great strength, like the willow tree that bends with the wind. It does not mean being submissive or fragile. It is taking responsibility of what we can control and having the strength to endure what is beyond our control. In times of great difficulty, acceptance is the first step toward progress.

The Darkest Hours

The darkness is upon you,
As it has been so many times before.
You remember yesterday
And all that it has brought you.
You look into tomorrow
And wonder what's in store.

The day is done.
The night has now begun.

From the eerie night, your dreams run wild,
Making spirit sore and anxieties compile
With thoughts of fear and sorrow.
Oh, these darkest hours, only a break in time
To test your spirit and your mind
In preparation for tomorrow.

During this temporary state,
While conscience lies in wait,
Allow yourself to be replenished.
Unleash your mind
From the burdens of the day.
Use this time to remind yourself
Things will be okay.

Appreciate the darkness.
You know it cannot last.
Time comes and goes so fast.

Brief is the moment of darkness,
Compared to the blinding light.
Embrace the darkness.
Do not fear the night.

From these darkest hours,
Build strength and courage
To face a brighter day.
Be ready for the morning.
The dawn is on its way.

Central to Buddhism is the Buddha's realization of four truths: 1) Life is suffering, 2) Suffering is caused by craving, 3) Suffering can have an end, and 4) There is a path that leads to the end of suffering. Darkness represents suffering. There are many forms of suffering. Negative emotions, including loneliness, depression, and hate, cause discomfort and pain. These emotions are reactions to experiences we encounter. The suffering is caused by the emotional reaction, not the experience. It is easy to blame the situation for our reaction. Instead of finding blame or excuses for our situation, perhaps we can look for the best response to better ourselves. Often, suffering is seen as some karmic punishment. This can create a sentiment of blaming victims; if something bad happens, it was a self-imposed reflection of thoughts or behaviors. People get understandably defensive when they think someone is telling them the bad things that happen to them are a punishment for something they did. Karma is not punishment and reward; it is cause and effect. Bad things do happen to good people. How we react to them can either enrich our lives or hinder our progress. We all go through dark times. That experience can be different for everyone. By embracing our experiences, good and bad, and learning from them, we find that we can grow from any situation. As we do, the darkness becomes just a cycle of life. We do not need to fear. As we grow through the darkness, we gain a greater appreciation for the light. The more we appreciate, the more we seem to have to appreciate.

Rise and Shine

Declaring war,
Dawn attacks the dying night.
Crawling over the horizon
Comes the army of growing light.

As trumpets sound,
From darkness you awake
To find the night's been captured
And the day is yours to take.

Armed with strength and courage
That night has given you,
You are prepared
To do what you must do.

It is time to rise and shine.
The day has now advanced.
While threatening your demise,
It still offers you a chance.

To take the spoils of the day,
You plot your battle plan,
Calling on every ounce of wisdom
To make the best attack you can.

Striking out at what's to come,
Use all that you have learned.
With light now on your side,
Surely the tides have turned.

In dark of night,
You set your goals.
Your mental strength
Enriched your soul.

By light of day,
Work through life's chores.
You've made it through the darkest hours.
Now claim the day as yours!

Forgiveness – The act of excusing a mistake or offense.

It has always been my belief that "forgiveness" was the greatest teaching of Jesus. The crux of the Christian religion is that He died to forgive all of us for our sins. I believe His "life" was greater than His "death." The example that He *lived* showed the importance of forgiveness.

     The feelings we hold toward others affect us far more than those for whom we hold feelings. Love brings even more joy to ourselves than to those we love. Hate brings more pain to us than to those we hate. Unforgiving pain causes mental and physical dis-ease to those who harbor it. *Learning to forgive is the greatest exercise we can do for ourselves.* Sometimes it is even more difficult to forgive ourselves than it is to forgive others. Forgiveness is a form of acceptance. True forgiveness is unconditional. We do not have to understand or agree with others to forgive them. We do not need them to see that they did wrong. You can know that they did wrong and let it go. It is ego that makes it so difficult to make this happen. Being "right" will not make the pain go away. True forgiveness will.

Forgive and Receive

Acceptance allows us to receive.
Acceptance leads to forgiveness.
Forgiveness can be given and received.
It is an enormously powerful gift.
It can heal giver and receiver.
Forgiveness cleanses the soul.

Chapter Four - **Compassion**

Compassion is that which makes the heart of the good move at the pain of others. It crushes and destroys the pain of others; thus, it is called compassion. It is called compassion because it shelters and embraces the distressed.

—Buddha

The word compassion means to share suffering. This great virtue drives us to alleviate others' discomfort. The Golden Rule—"Do unto others as you would have them do unto you"—is an expression of compassion. This sentiment is echoed throughout most religions. This type of deep caring is a combination of respect and appreciation for life—our own and that of others. Compassion breeds charity, sharing, and giving of one's self.

Appreciation – Understanding the value of life, ourselves, and others as we exist in this moment.

Be content with what you have;
Rejoice in the way things are.
When you realize there is nothing lacking
The whole world belongs to you.

—Lao Tzu

Appreciation is recognizing value. In fact, when something is said to increase in value, it appreciates. A rare old coin buried in a jar has the same value as equal denominations. When it is recognized as special or rare, then its value increases. When we see every individual as unique—and therefore extremely rare—we can appreciate their value. Value leads to respect. Respect, seeing the divinity in others and in ourselves, creates a sense of equality and oneness. Respecting all life leads to compassion for all life. Compassion brings healing and wellness into the world. We all want to be appreciated, just as we all want to be loved. Knowing how good it feels should be enough reason to appreciate all we have.

Cost of Appreciation

Easier to want what I don't have
Than to appreciate what I do,
I often wonder why I can't acquire happiness
Or why my wishes don't come true.

When my wishes do come true,
I still do not change my attitude.
I just see more to wish for
Instead of gratitude.

When focusing on my wants,
It's difficult to see
All of the gifts
I already have received.

Gifts we take for granted
Are eventually taken away.
Value is more apparent
When loss is the price we pay.

So happiness comes from loss,
Or so it would seem.
Until we are happy for *all* we have,
Happiness is still a dream.

I have learned to have a greater appreciation for the food I eat. I do not mean that I enjoy the flavors more; I have a deeper gratitude for the nourishment food provides me. This new gratitude has helped me to be more particular about which foods to ingest. It also seems to increase the nourishment I receive from every bite, allowing me to need less and receive more. Taking a moment before eating to consciously acknowledge my gratitude for the food I am about to consume increases my enjoyment of the food.

Respect – The state of being regarded in honor or high esteem.

Namaste is a greeting of respect. It is interpreted from Hindi to mean, "The divinity in me perceives and adores the divinity in you." What a beautiful expression. Divinity, or qualities of God, can be seen in all things, including ourselves. Self-respect can protect us from emotional harm. We can love even those who treat us badly without allowing them to hurt us. In order to respect others, it helps to see life through their eyes. In any situation, putting ourselves in others' positions can help us understand them. Even if we do not agree with others, seeing the divinity within them allows us to respect them and accept them as they are.

Smile in Your Eyes

There is a smile in your eyes.
I see words behind the smile.
Still, I cannot read what it is saying.
What does it mean?
Please, spell it out for me.

How can I know what you are thinking
Or what your face is trying to say?
Let me know where you are heading.
Allow me to help you find the way.

Open up your heart.
Verbalize your feelings.
Let the words fall from your lips.
My ears are always open.
I'll listen very carefully
And respond to you
In truest honesty.

My mind is not to judge
Or sway you from your thoughts.
I am learning of self-understanding
And teach what I am being taught.

Free yourself from mental bondage.
As your friend, I'll share your burden.
Speak openly to me.
Worry not for gentle wording.

Release to me your fears and sorrows.
I'll ease your soul into tomorrow.

I will not let you hang on knotted rope
Or let you suffer from loss of hope.

Your facial expression is a mere façade.
There is a smile in your eyes.
Is it just a shield
For you to hide behind?

You need no protection.
I hold no sword or dagger.
I'll guide you in a straight line
If you should begin to stagger.

Confide in me, my friend.
I'll support you through the end.

Respect is born of love. From birth, the way we are treated by our parents develops our learning patterns. Healthy respect is cultivated during childhood. We learn what we live. When tyranny is used in the attempt to elicit respect, the result is *fear* and *resistance*. Only *love* can create respect and acceptance. *Teaching children to love themselves is the greatest gift we can give.* Self-respect determines our capacity to respect others. When we see the divinity in *all, we* build unity.

Chapter Five - **Truth**

Truth has many meanings and many theories. The word can be used in different contexts. In human relations, truth can mean honesty and integrity. In science, it can be an accepted fact. On a spiritual level, truth describes All That Is. This meaning is described in the American Heritage dictionary as "an ideal or fundamental reality apart from and transcending perceived experience: the basic truths of life." Universal truth may contradict scientific truth and supersede human understanding. As science continues to expand its understanding of the universe, many once accepted truths are now being questioned within the scientific community. In this context, "truth" changes, or at least what we believe to be truth changes as we continue to explore and learn. The Buddha says the same of our understanding of spiritual truth. As we begin to understand it, it evolves. We will continue to learn truth for eternity.

As a virtue, truth is paramount. We cannot develop true relationships based on lies. A weak foundation cannot support a stable structure. Living in lies demonstrates a lack of faith in universal truth. Believing we can create a reality outside of truth is not only futile, it is self-destructive. Accepting truth is necessary to be in harmony with the universe. Sharing truth builds healthy foundations and strong relationships.

As a universal or spiritual concept, truth is omniscient. Truth sees all and knows all. It is all-encompassing. Nothing exists outside of truth. We are not able to comprehend it fully. We do not need to. We simply need to understand that it exists and we are part of it. Recognizing truth in every aspect of our life and incorporating it in all our choices accelerates our self-actualization. Our journey of enlightenment is our search for truth. When we lie to ourselves or others, we are turning away from truth. When we turn our backs to the light of truth, we look into darkness. Truth is the light. The light is our guide.

House of Cards

A house of cards
Is a remarkable creation.
Like a life of lies,
It has no foundation.

You need to tiptoe
As you walk around
To protect your house
From tumbling down.

You know what I am saying
If I am talking about you.
You are living in lies,
And you know it is true.

Someday, truth will come
Like the winds of change.
The house you built
Will be rearranged.

We build what we live
And live what we build.

If you build with lies,
It will all come down
When truth blows in
And knocks it to the ground.

When you start all over,
Will you do it again?
To build with truth
Is a choice from within.

We can build with love
Or we can build with hate.
Each of us builds
Our own fate.

My goal is to remain in a state of joy. The greatest joy is love. Giving and receiving love can bring joy. There are different ways to give and receive love. It is fundamental to love yourself and to love life in order to truly love others. There are many parallels to loving others, self, and life. The same virtues are required for any type of love. Unconditional love is what we aim to give. It is not dependent on what we receive. As long as we can give love to ourselves, we can love others without *needing* to be loved in return. We cannot demand love from anyone. We can only control what we give. We can have enough love for ourselves that we draw in more love and repel harmful emotion and behavior.

We try so hard to receive love from others. We have little control of what we receive and total control of what we give. We can give love to others and to ourselves. If we focus on the love we give, we can apply love to all that we receive. That is the key to opening ourselves to receive. As we do, we have more to give. Giving and receiving are an escalating perpetual cycle.

The law of cause and effect is one of the most outstanding truths of the universe. We get what we give. This truth gives us control of our own lives. The most important truth is that we can each connect directly to The Source. We do not need another person to interpret God's will for us. We can learn to listen to our Divine Voice. By opening our hearts and minds, we can receive direct personal guidance from The Great Spirit. We can all become "conscious co-creators."

Part Three

Moving Forward

When I was a senior in high school, we were given the option of adding a quote under our picture in the yearbook. I chose the following: "Learn from yesterday, plan for tomorrow, and live for today." At the time, I did not realize how important that concept truly is. It is these three actions that determine what we make of our life. Letting go of the past is the first step in moving forward on our journey. Our past is the path that led us to our present. Any variation could have altered who we are today. We can do nothing to change the past. By accepting and forgiving the past, we are able to learn and grow from it. Good or bad, when we let go,we grow. We can learn from our mistakes as well as our successes. It is good to remember both, but not to cling to either. Planning is the second step in the process of creating our future. It is thought. Exercising our free will during this crucial step is the key to consciously creating our own future. We choose what that thought will be. It makes sense to want positive thoughts. We control our thoughts. Regardless of our situation, only we choose our thoughts. Our thoughts become our reality. The third step is being in the now. It is doing, taking action. Our only reality is this very moment. Our present is a culmination of all our past experiences and the creation point for our future. By drawing a line from where we were to where we are, we predict where we are heading. Moving forward is letting go of the past and creating our future by living in the now.

Chapter Six - **Letting Go**

I use the term "letting go" in reference to all attachments—ego, control, possessions, the past, and even people. Our fear of loss deludes us into believing we have the power to hold on forever. By holding on, we are preventing ourselves from moving forward. We cannot change the past. We can learn from it and try our best not to repeat the same mistakes we have made before. No possession will last forever. Hoarding is a reaction to a fear of lacking. Controlling others is a detriment to them and to us. The only thing we need to control is our own free will. Ego is an illusionary veil that separates us from all that is. I like the fundamental message of "letting go" of attachments, not just attachment to material things, but to emotions and paradigms. A major challenge is letting go of ego.

Ego

The *American Heritage* dictionary defines "ego" as "the 'I' or self of any person; a person as thinking, feeling, and willing, and distinguishing itself from the selves of others and from objects of its thoughts." This separation is only in our minds. We have developed this pattern of understanding ourselves and everything we perceive. When we shift that paradigm and look instead for the connections, we can allow ourselves to see from other perspectives. Seeing ourselves through another's eyes affords us a better, more complete view of our true condition—a state of unity.

The primary function of ego is self-preservation. The ego protects *itself* over protecting the *whole* being. Shedding the protective layer of ego is an evolutionary process. Seeing ourselves as separate from the world around us was an important defense mechanism for the propagation of our species. Humans have evolved to the top of the food chain. Now, other humans are our only predators. We see others as competition, and therefore, as a threat. When we shed our ego and see ourselves as connected to The Source and to all things, we no longer need to compete for survival. This evolution is a threat to the existence of ego. In defense, ego tries to convince our conscious mind to fear. By letting go of these fears, our ego is no longer needed to protect us.

Allow

As part of allowing,
We let go of ego
To find our true selves
As part of the whole.

Letting go of ego is not about possessions,
As much as mental perception.
It is not about controlling our "need for attention."
It is no longer needing to be right
or others' confirmations.

I am here. I am now.
I will continue to allow.

The more I let go,
The more free I become.

All that I receive
Is meant for me,
While nothing is mine to own.

No thought or thing is mine alone,
Yet all I am and all I have
I alone have chosen.

Attachments

Letting go of attachments to vices is a common theme in major religions. For Catholics, the largest sect of Christianity, Ash Wednesday marks the beginning of Lent. The purpose of this forty-day-long event is to prepare, through prayer, penitence, almsgiving, and self-denial, for the annual commemoration of the death and resurrection of Jesus. These practices, which are intended to encourage spiritual growth, could also be called meditation, forgiveness, charity, and abstinence. Regardless of religious belief, these disciplines each have obvious merit for enriching one's soul. Lent is most commonly known as a time of asceticism. The adjective "ascetic" derives from the ancient Greek term *askesis*, meaning "practice, training, or exercise." Originally associated with any form of disciplined practice, the term "ascetic" has come to mean anyone who practices a renunciation of worldly pursuits to achieve higher intellectual and spiritual goals. The purpose of practicing an ascetic lifestyle is not merely to be virtuous, but to prepare for mind-body transformation. The founders and early practitioners of some forms of Christianity, Buddhism, and Hinduism refrained from many physical pleasures and the accumulation of material wealth. They believed wealth and pleasures of the flesh were distractions from spiritual pursuit. Most people in our society would consider asceticism as extreme; however, it can have great benefits, such as simplicity and peacefulness of mind. Material wealth often comes with stress and a lack of free time for personal development.

As with most holidays, Lent is a symbolic gesture. It reminds us of spiritual exercises practiced by the most revered spiritual leaders. Although I do not consider myself a religious person, I am a highly spiritual person. I embrace any discipline that encourages my own spiritual growth. Letting go of attachments is a personal goal I have set for myself. This does not mean I do not allow myself to enjoy possessions or indulging in pleasures of the flesh, including food and alcohol. It is only the attachment or addiction to these things that I resist. Observing Lent is a good way to address our addictions or attachments and prove to ourselves that our free will is more powerful than our urges. Although I am not usually a proponent of ritual, I appreciate the value of this religious holiday.

Letting go of attachments can be a difficult challenge for many of us. Giving up all personal belongings may seem extreme. At what level are we comfortable in letting go? To "let go" does not necessarily mean to discard. It just means not to clench onto. Understanding that *no* thing belongs to us and that *every* thing is temporary empowers us to find joy in *all* things. When we can fully appreciate that which is before us in the moment, we become free to attract greater experiences. Without trying to control our environment, we are open to the highest good.

Giving up attachments can be very liberating; however, austerity itself can become an attachment. Buddha did not become enlightened until he realized this for himself. Siddhartha Guatama was born around 563 BC. According to the traditional biography, his father was King Suddhodana. He was given the name Siddhartha, meaning "the one who achieves his aim." After examining the infant, the hermit seer Asita announced that the child would become *either* a great king *or* a great holy man. Wanting his son to be a great king, *not* a holy man, the king shielded his son from religious teachings or knowledge of human suffering. He built three palaces to isolate him from the outside world. When he was twenty-nine, Siddhartha went out to meet his subjects. His father did his best to hide those who were old, sick, or suffering. When he saw an old man, his charioteer explained that all people get old. Later, he saw a rotting corpse, a diseased man, and an ascetic. When he discovered the poverty and disease that existed in the kingdom outside the walls of his palace, he renounced his life of wealth and luxury for one of asceticism. Giving up all his belongings, Siddhartha turned to begging for alms in the street. In search of enlightenment, he pushed his austerities even further by practicing deprivation of nearly all worldly goods. One day, after nearly starving himself to death, he collapsed in a river while bathing and nearly drowned. After that, Siddhartha began to reconsider his path. Upon deep meditation, he discovered what Buddhists now refer to as "The Middle Way," moderation between self-indulgence and self-mortification. He found in his quest to give up attachments that asceticism had become a crutch and was keeping him from enlightenment just as much as the wealth had. After forty-nine days of meditation, at age thirty-five, Siddhartha Guatama attained enlightenment. From that point on, he was known as "The Awakened One."

People

The people in our lives reflect who we are. In different phases of our life, we may attract different types of people. As we grow and evolve as individuals, the people in our lives will grow with us, fade away, or hold us back. We can influence others, but we cannot change them. Change can only come from within. If we make the conscious choice to improve ourselves, we may also have to make choices about the people with whom we associate. This is not always easy. We do not want to leave behind the ones we love. If they are not ready to make the same choice to evolve, we either allow them to keep us from our own goals or separate ourselves enough so we have room to move toward our personal goals. As we achieve our goals, we can offer encouragement and guidance. In any recovery or self-improvement program, it is recommended to separate one's self from the people who you are used to being around because it is often those people that were involved with the behaviors you are working to overcome. Any successful person will tell you they surround themselves with like-minded people. When positively motivated people surround us, we lift each other up and propel each other forward. Wanting the best for others attracts those who want the best for us. Operating from a place of limitless possibility, we do not need to compete to be successful. We can rejoice in the success of others.

Our society does not promote the idea of limitless potential. We tend to act from a state of lacking. We are taught to think another's success diminishes our own. We measure our level of success or failure by comparison to others. This is the cause of the crab-in-a-bucket theory. The crab-in-a-bucket theory refers to the behavior of crabs when placed inside a bucket. While a single crab may find a way to escape, when several crabs are put in a bucket, none will escape. As one crab claws its way to the top, the others will pull it back down. This is a true phenomenon. Crab mentality is also a metaphor for the human response to self-improvement in others. Often, when people see others advancing themselves, they subconsciously reach out to hold them back.

John and Matt had been friends for a long time. They went to bars to drink and pick up women a few nights every week. They would laugh about being hungover and calling in sick for work. They did not have meaningful relationships. Women were merely conquests. Eventually, Matt began to see the harm he was doing to himself physically, emotionally, and spiritually. He was sacrificing so many goals and desires for the same shallow experiences week after week. He decided he wanted to make a change. He told John he did not want to behave like that anymore. Instead of encouraging Matt to better himself, John took it as an insult. He saw nothing wrong with the social rut they had dug for themselves. He was comfortable with the way things were. He did not want change. John tried to drag Matt down any way he could. He even used guilt to try to keep Matt from changing. Subconsciously, he was afraid that if Matt found happiness elsewhere, it would reflect a weakness in him. Instead of seeing an opportunity for personal growth, he chose to hold his friend back. Does this sound familiar to you? Have you ever been in Matt or John's position?

It is not always a friend who holds us back—it can even be an intimate partner or family member. In that case, it can be more difficult to let go. People tend to hold on tightly when a person they love or care for deeply is trying to grow; if we are the one trying to make changes, the people closest to us may hold on to us so tightly that pulling away is very hard. Whether it is someone who continues to hurt us or himself, does not fulfill our needs, or simply chooses to move on, we can learn to let go. When we do, we allow ourselves an opportunity for growth. If we do not, we only hurt ourselves and the other person.

Love is a Bird in the Hand

God gave to the dove
A special gift.
With wings she was born.
To be free like the wind,
She need only give them a lift.

The dove need never fight,
For she was given the gift of flight.
Loving and peaceful
Is the bird of pure white.
But soft and fragile is the creature
That does not fight.

Love too is free,
Always in search
For somewhere to be.

To hold a dove
Gently in your hand
Is to have the warmth
Of love in your heart.

Once in your hand,
Only you control the dove.
Seeded in your heart,
Try you to control the love.

Happy are you to have the dove.
Happy are you to be in love.

Take care as not to let go.
Open your hand
And away it will fly.

Reach for the bird
And the farther it goes.
This will not happen again
Because now the hand knows.

In time, another dove passes.
Into your hand it flies.
Onto this dove your hand holds tight.
This bird will not return to flight.

Squeeze tighter do you
As the bird tries to fly.
Even harder you squeeze
As you watch the dove die.

By trying to hold on too tight we are demonstrating fear and lack of faith. It is a futile attempt to control. Manipulating a person or situation through force only creates resistance. Resistance to the flow of life demonstrates a lack of faith and prevents growth. It is arrogant to believe that only we know what is best for the higher good. By allowing ourselves to experience without fear and need to control, we invite greater experiences into our lives.

Waiting for Another

When will you ever learn?
What does it take for you to understand?
You had love in the palm of your hand.

In your hand,
she was happy to stay.
But still you feared
She would fly away.

You squeezed her hard,
And you made her cry.
You squeezed her harder,
And you watched her die.
Now forever the dove will rest
Lying lifeless in your trembling fist.

Even with no breath of life remaining,
Your hand is still unsure,
Until the day you can stand
The death of love no more.

Realizing the loss of love
You have incurred,
You promise yourself
A love that's pure.

So, once again, your hand is open and
Your palm is facing toward the sun,
Looking for a dove
To be your only one.

Time passes
Like clouds on a windless day.

Not a day goes by
That you don't pray
To find a love
Forever with you to stay.

Safe and inviting,
Your hand has become
A resting place
For birds on the run.

Offering freedom
To come and go as they please,
You no longer find yourself
Trying to squeeze.

One by one,
You hold each bird,
No sacrifices
or promises offered.

Wanting never
to hurt another again,
You know in the end
You will have to win.

So you go on waiting
And knowing you will find
A dove that will stay
Loving and kind.

Just keep on waiting.
You know you will find
A dove out there searching
For a hand like yours,
One that's always open, loving, and kind.

Learning to "let go" has been one of many ongoing lessons for me. If we are holding something tightly in our hand, our hand is not open for something better. Even after writing about it, it took a long time for me to understand this. I started writing poetry as a preteen. I was a senior in high school when I realized how important writing was to me. In Mrs. Heisey's Rock Poetry class, we were interpreting lyrics from rock music. The line "love is a bird in the hand" grew from class discussion to my first poem on relationships. It opened up a floodgate of writing. I had found my new outlet. It was therapeutic. Soon, I began using writing to explore my spirituality. One quote sparked a poem that would become the title for this book and the foundation of my spiritual beliefs. I started to see a pattern in my poems. I was defining my own understanding of life. I decided I wanted to compile my writings into a book to clarify my feelings for myself and to share with others. I learned so much between the time when I decided what I wanted and when I finally knew what I had to do.

Paradigms

Another aspect of letting go is releasing old paradigms or patterns of thought. As I began to learn and grow spiritually, mostly through my relationships with others, I began to notice repeating patterns in my relationships. I had thought it would be enough to recognize what I had learned from my experiences. I figured writing down the lessons would get me beyond the experience. Repeating the same types of situations over and over frustrated me. I did not know how to change.

Words Unlearned

I know these words.
I've read them countless times.
I wrote these words.
I thought I understood them.
I feel the words.
I lived them time and time again.
I speak the words.
I wish I could get beyond them.
How do I put the words behind me
When the feelings still live inside?
What good is it to know my feelings,
To see them and to label them with words?
Why must I relive the same
Painful experiences over and over?
Have I not learned what I need to know?
I've written down my lessons.
What more do I have to learn?
Have I missed a lesson
Or just not completely learned
The lessons of my experience?

Learning not to beat ourselves up for our own behavior helps us to not be so hard on others. A lot of the stuff I was telling myself to do fifteen years ago I am still not doing. Although I am working harder to improve, I do not expect to be perfect overnight. I no longer aim to find perfection. Instead, I find happiness with every forward step. Finding great joy in our progress, we accept our stumbles. We have to understand the difficulty of staying on the path so we can relate to others we might help along the way. The most destructive paradigm we must overcome is fear. The next is judgment. Judgment fogs vision. Learning to observe without judgment gives greater perception. Releasing preconceived thought opens the mind to new possibilities.

The mind is like a parachute. It only works when it is open.
—Frank Zappa

Fear/Dis-ease

In 1995, I studied *The Art of Becoming* by Dr. Gene Basin. He taught two powerful techniques that anyone can use to sculpt the condition of his or her life. The first is used to heal us from our past. Healing our past is a four-step process. First, we must identify the symptoms from which we are suffering. The second step is to understand the paradigm associated with the symptoms. Suffering, whether from addiction, physical illness, or depression, is the result of thought patterns from our subconscious mind. Louise L. Hay's book *You Can Heal Your Life* has an excellent index for dis-ease and the thought patterns that contribute to it. The third step is to remember the events that caused us to form these beliefs. Through contemplation and the use of hypnosis or meditation, an individual can pinpoint memories of the past, which our higher conscious can relate to these beliefs. It is not uncommon for many memories to cause the same feelings. The next step is the most important—we forgive. We forgive the person who we felt had wronged us, we forgive the situation, and we forgive ourselves for getting into the situation. By releasing judgment of the incident, we are no longer bound to it. We are free. As part of forgiving, we end by reading an affirmation from the index.

In my case, I was suffering from hemorrhoids. I looked in Louise Hay's dis-ease index. She listed "fear of deadlines, anger of the past, afraid to let go, and feeling burdened" as causes. It is no wonder this problem often affects taxi drivers and delivery people; it is not about sitting as much as the race against the clock. When I thought about anxiety in relation to my condition, I instantly remembered being in my bedroom only a couple of days earlier. I had been startled by a pounding on the front door. When I went to investigate, I found an eviction notice nailed to the front door. My roommate had failed to give all the rent to the landlord, and I was anxious that he would not take care of it in time to prevent us from being thrown out. The teacher who was guiding me through the book helped me to forgive my roommate and release him from judgment. He then asked me to do the same for myself and for the situation as a whole. I released my fear of eviction along with the blame I was holding toward my roommate. I then repeated the following affirmation: "I release all that is unlike love. There is time and space for everything I want to do."
Within minutes, I felt relief from the discomfort I had been feeling for weeks. By the next day, my hemorrhoids were completely gone. It was embarrassing to talk about it then. By accepting it consciously and addressing it on a deeper subconscious level, I was able to put a major "pain in the ass" behind me and move forward without fear or judgment.

The Past

I spent many years floating aimlessly in the sea of life with no anchor and no direction. I stopped writing. I put my spiritual growth on hold. I did not understand why I was not getting anywhere. One day, I woke up and realized a lot had happened in ten years, but not much had changed. My life had been on autopilot for a while. Although it was a fun ride, I felt like I was waking up from an exciting dream. Trying to hold onto the dream did not work. Finally,

I got out of bed to take on the day at hand. As my intention changed and I regained direction in my life, I accepted my past and was ready to move forward once again. I wondered what lessons I could learn from my hiatus. I pondered how I could grow from the experience.

One night, I went to bed thinking about *why* I had stopped writing for so long. I also appreciated how nice it was to be reading again and writing new material. It was like being reunited with an old friend—me. I could see how much I still had in common with my old writings. I also saw how much I had grown. I believe several factors caused me to stop expressing myself through poetry and prose. Fear and anger became stumbling blocks. By recognizing these obstacles, I was able to overcome them.

My first setback hit me after a great revelation. In 1993, I had just learned about Kundalini meditation. It is a very powerful way to connect the conscious mind to the higher self and Godhead. It can be dangerous if the proper precautions are not taken. When done correctly, it can open the mind to its full potential. In an overwhelming *ah-ha* moment, I gained an incredible feeling of personal responsibility for the condition of my life. Anything that happened to me was created by me. My reaction to any situation determined how it would affect me. I also believed that my knowing made me more responsible for my karma and the Law of Attraction. Although in the American judicial system ignorance of the law is not a defense, I thought if I did not know the laws of nature, I could not be held responsible to obey them. I believed understanding karma made me more responsible to its effects. If someone who understands karma steals, the karmic effect is greater than it would be for someone who had never been made conscious of the universal laws of cause and effect. For example, if someone who did not understand stole $20, they might lose or have stolen the equivalent amount. If I stole $20, I might lose or have stolen $100. Whether this extra responsibility was true or not, I stuck my head in the sand to separate myself from what I believed. This was ego protecting it its most basic form. By definition, that is what ego does—separate self from all else.

When I realized what my ego was doing to me, I was very hard on myself, though I am trying to be more forgiving now. At the time, I was stuck in a learning-teaching paradox. I wanted to learn. I knew the best way to learn was the same as the best way to teach—by doing. I felt like I could not write or even say what I believed to be right or wrong if I was not doing it myself. How could I say we should treat our bodies as a temple if I continued to put harmful substances in my own? How could I write on the importance of patience if I got angry with slow drivers in the fast lane? How could I speak on the importance of letting go of attachments when I had so many? Most of all, how could I write on the evil of hypocrisy? Would I have to become a saint or Buddha before I could share my writing or even talk about what I believed? Instead, I decided I could be an intern, a working student. I could write down these lessons I have learned, even if I have not mastered them. I could use these writings as a goal for where I would like to be. Most of all, by writing, I am being what I want to be. In *being*, I am fulfilling my greatest purpose to myself.

Another hurdle I set for myself was fear of failure. I knew I had good insights to share. What if no one else enjoyed hearing them from me? If I did not share, I would never have to know. Procrastination for the purpose of living in *potential* is not living in the now. Instead of living my dream, I thought it might be easier to prove my ability to build financial success first. Living in this material mentality, I built a wall between myself and the progression of my writing and my own awareness of me. It started with a plan. I convinced myself it was the best plan for my *future*. I figured out what I wanted and how to get there *someday*. I wanted a business that was in line with my spiritual and philosophical beliefs. My dream was to open a wellness center. I thought if I could own a wellness center, I would be surrounded by like-minded people. I hoped it would give me the freedom to spend my time writing, while my holistic business would run itself. I convinced myself that if I could get enough money to open it, I would be successful and happy. I did not want a partner. Perhaps my ego thought I could make all the right decisions. I had no credit. I was making a living by selling hair wraps to tourists. I had worked for a man who became a millionaire by selling them at Disney resorts. I was supporting myself with my Bohemian business. If I could do what he was doing, I would have enough to open the business of my dreams. Instead of doing what I ultimately wanted to do, which was to write, I devised a plan to make money in another way so that *someday* I could afford to write and not have to work. I could have continued "getting by" and been able to write in my abundant free time. I had no spouse or kids. I did not even own a TV. If I had done it differently, I might have lost so many of the wonderful memories I have today. I might have never met my amazing wife. But I am doing it now. Now is *all* that matters.

My plan was a subconscious procrastination. I was delaying my own joy. At the time, I did not understand what I was doing. I only recently discovered what I believe to be some of the possible underlying causes for my subconscious behavior. I was forced to accept a new realization: To forge the reality I truly wanted to create, I had to accept personal responsibility and face possible failure. I got up out of bed to write down this epiphany: "It may be easier to live in potential greatness than to risk potential failure, yet only through risk can we realize greatness." I was no longer afraid to attempt living my dream. Instead, I started doing it.

Doing is a constant theme in my life. By doing we teach and learn. More importantly, *doing* is the essence of living. It is the process of doing that keeps us in the now. *Planning* to do is living in potential. Doing is the goal. The outcome of the doing is less relevant than the act of doing. I enjoy painting. The process of painting is enjoyable. I would like to create something beautiful, but it is the *act* of painting that I find so enjoyable. I feel the same way about writing. I enjoy writing. I would like to write something meaningful; however, the end result is less important than the process itself.

The final obstacle was set on a very beautiful summer day in 1993. I had always believed the age of twenty-three would be the prime of my life, even though I had always heard it was nineteen. I figured I needed an extra four years of maturity. Just as most men of that age do, I thought I knew a lot more than I probably did. Maybe I did feel more self-aware than many other guys. But fearing that I may have hit my peak seems silly looking back now. I was enjoying a simple, but fun and easy, life. On that day in 1993, I was taking a very special girl to a very special place.

Playa Linda beach is on the National Seashore in Titusville, Florida. It is about forty-five minutes east of Orlando. The only man-made structure that can be seen from the beach is the docking station for the space shuttle launches. In Spanish, the word for "beach" is *playa* and the word for "beautiful" is *Linda*. Even the long drive from the entrance of the state park to the beach parking access road is surrounded in beauty. We picked our spot and laid out our blanket. She took me by the hand and led me slowly toward the water. Holding hands, we walked down the beach, feeling like the only two people on it. It was an incredible day for both of us. It made me think of a poem I had written a few years earlier. I titled it "Moon Lit." I stopped her and turned back toward the blanket. I looked forward to reading her the poem.

When we got close to the blanket, we were confused. Where did all our stuff go? Her bag was gone. My bag, with my car keys and wallet, was gone. The only thing on the blanket was a towel and our shoes. What upset me most was the devastation I saw in her eyes. Along with wondering how I was going to get us home and then get back to the beach the next day to pick up my car—plus the ordeal of replacing the contents of my wallet, I felt terrible for her. To make it worse, she informed me that her mother had given her a watch on her sixteenth birthday, the year before her passing. It was the last gift she ever received from her mother, and she had left in her bag. All she could do was cry. I could not believe such a great day could go so wrong. I was so devastated I did not fully acknowledge the kindness of the stranger who brought us home.

Once home, I decided to sort out my feelings by writing about the experience. That was when I realized all my poetry had been taken from me. Two books filled with notes and thoughts that I had recorded were gone. Although I had copies of many of my favorite poems, many more had not been copied elsewhere. So many random thoughts were lost. I could not understand why something like that had happened to us. What did that say about our karma, about *my* karma? It hurt for a long time. I felt so violated. My friend was in no hurry to go out with me again, either. I did not know if she blamed me or if she was scared to go back out with me. It was difficult to write again after that. I wondered if perhaps I had failed the test. I was crushed.

Nevertheless, we did stay in touch. She remains a very good friend to this day. A few years after the event, she was shopping and saw an exact copy of the watch her mother had bought nearly seven years before. It was an amazing find, which she took as a good sign from her mom. Though she did not have the original, she now had one that looked just like it. I was relieved from the guilt I had felt.

For a long time, I hoped that somehow I would be reunited with my journals. It took a lot to let go and put the experience behind me. It was time to move on. It was time for change.

Chapter Seven - **Creating Our Future**

Visions are like objects in the distance, the closer we move toward them, the clearer they become.
—Author unknown

In my past, similar situations often repeated themselves. Different reactions, on my part, led to equally different outcomes. In learning the mechanics of relationships, I was inadvertently learning to drive my own experiences. I was not always able to avoid unwanted situations, but I could determine the effect an episode would have on me by how I would react. I was becoming aware that I was, and always had been, the captain of my own ship. No longer would I be stuck floating aimlessly in the endless sea of life.

The power of creation begins with thought. Sending thought into the universe is like placing an order for delivery. Good or bad, our thoughts will soon manifest and return to us. Speaking or writing our thoughts adds priority to our order. It seems to manifest quicker. Taking action on our thoughts is like picking up the order ourselves. For example, I can go online to order a book to be mailed to me. I will need to allow two to four weeks for delivery. For a few extra dollars, I can have it "rush delivered" in a matter of days. Or I can go to the bookstore and have it the same day. This is the difference between creating with thoughts, words, or actions. How much thought do we put into ordering food for delivery? First, we think of what type of food we desire. Next, we choose a restaurant. Then we decide which meal. Finally, we decide if we want to pay extra and wait a little longer for delivery or if we should go pick it up ourselves. Do we use this same conscious effort with our *choice* of thoughts, words, and actions we use throughout our day?

When I was younger, I told my stepmother I was so "anxious" to begin summer camp that I just couldn't wait. She corrected me, explaining that anxious means nervous, not excited. The word I was looking for was "eager." I have been very conscious of the difference ever since. I hear other people misuse the word, and it reminds me of that little lesson and a much bigger lesson I learned later.

I no longer use the phrase "I can't wait" for anything. Instead I say, "I am looking forward to…" since "I can't wait" implies a lack of patience. Patience is a virtue I am improving within myself. Also, I prefer to use the positive affirmation of "looking forward" rather than the negative connotation of not having the ability to wait. "Looking forward" implies a positive vision for the future. I have taken the phrase "I can't" out of my vocabulary. Instead, I may say, "I currently struggle with…" or "I am getting better at…" In the case of patience, I do not say, "I have a problem with patience." I say, "I am improving my patience." This simple change is an example of consciously changing my creative power with thoughts and words.

This same practice can be done with any negative thoughts. Some negative thoughts are more difficult to address. Negative thoughts toward others often originate as judgment. Many of us are quick to judge others, either mentally or verbally. Learning to tolerate and respect people who believe and act differently begins by consciously exercising being nonjudgmental. Training ourselves to recognize our similarities to others instead of our differences builds an instant bond to them instead of a barrier. This helps build new relationships. It also helps with internal growth by recognizing in others what they might have to teach us about ourselves. Seeing every contact with another person as an opportunity to learn about ourselves is one way perspective can create growth from a challenge. It is easy to rationalize negative thoughts that are provoked by others. Although more challenging, learning not to be drawn into others' negativity is an opportunity to strengthen our own positive energy and demonstrate positive behavior to others. The simple exercise of recognizing negative thoughts or behaviors will lead to replacing them with positive ones.

Because we are a part of the whole, we influence it and vice versa. Just as our fingers are a part of our body, we are a part of the universe. If we cut our finger, messages are sent to the whole body for assistance. First, an immediate message is sent to the brain in the form of pain. This allows us to react to the situation to protect ourselves from further injury and to address the one sustained. While we are consciously caring for the wound with compression to stop the bleeding, our body's internal response has already begun. Platelets in the blood begin clotting the area to reduce blood loss. Neurological inhibitors are produced to help with the pain. White blood cells rush to the area to fight bacteria. The different systems of our bodies communicate chemically through the blood and electronically through the nervous system. All parts of the body work together. As individuals, we communicate and interact with the world around us as an integral part of the system. Being conscious of what we choose to communicate empowers us to choose more wisely.

I learned one of my favorite exercises in manifestation from Dr. Wayne W. Dyer. It is simple and fast acting. The last thoughts in our minds before we go to sleep at night are replayed over and over throughout the night. If we go to sleep worried about an event happening the next day, our minds worry all night. That sends a message of fear to the universe. If we look at the same event and think, "Tomorrow I will have a great opportunity to address and resolve an issue," we are telling the universe that we have faith that we will be okay. Whichever message we send out, the universe will send back to us; in essence, the universe proves us right. In the last five minutes before going to sleep, we can easily find five things for which to be thankful. We can also be thankful for the great opportunities that will present themselves the next day. This simple exercise makes sleep much more restful. It also makes for a much better day to come. As with any new habit, after just one month it will become second nature. In that time, I believe you will see incredible results, which will encourage you to continue.

Affirmations

Louise L. Hay is one of the most influential authors in my life. She exemplifies all the concepts I have outlined in this book. She took control of her own life and created radical change. After self-publishing her first book, she went on to build Hay House Publications, the leading publishing house for spiritual development. Her first book was *You Can Heal Your Body*. Soon after, she revised and expanded it with her release of *You Can Heal Your Life*. She effectively teaches the use of affirmations to program our thought patterns to draw health, happiness, and prosperity into our lives. Affirmations are clear, simple phrases we can read to ourselves or say out loud to convey the messages we wish to send into the universe, and therefore, draw onto our lives. Repeating affirmations is an easy, practical method to consciously change our thought patterns, and therefore, change our life. In her books, she compiled an incredible index of affirmations that correlate thoughts with their respective effects. She has affirmations to help with virtually every aspect of well-being. My personal favorite affirmation is the following: "In my thoughts, words, and actions, I am creating the life I have always dreamed of living."

When I was attending Florida College of Natural Health, one of the administrators told me a story of her "successful" affirmation. She had been pulled over by the police several times in just a few months. She felt like they were picking her out, while others were driving much faster than her. She began repeating an affirmation every day: "I am invisible to the police; they cannot see me." In doing so, she also became more conscious of her own driving and those around her. One day, she was stopped at a light. She had come to a full stop. A few seconds later, she felt a tremendous jolt that slammed her into her steering wheel and fractured her ankle. Before she knew what happened, a cop ran up to her window and asked if she was all right. He said he was very sorry. He saw the light, but did not even see her car until it was too late. After that incident, she became much more conscious of the wording for her affirmations.

Imagination

What the mind of man can conceive and believe, it can achieve.
—Napoleon Hill

Soon after learning to heal my past, I learned the most powerful technique for healing from Dr. Gene Basin. He taught me how to construct my own future using creative imagery. Our imagination, or Divine Inspiration, is the creative force that designs the blueprint of our future. Imagination is the key to any creativity. As we practice, it becomes easier and we get better at it. To start, it is good to relax and clear our minds with a couple of deep breaths. Then we can begin by painting a picture in our minds. If we desire a new car, we first visualize the car we would like to have. We see the make, the model, the year, and the color of the car. Then we put ourselves in the vehicle. Being in your scenario is important. After all, it is *your* future you are creating. Now it starts to get really fun as we fill in the details. The more details we can create in our minds, the more effective this process becomes. For this we incorporate all our senses. Where are you driving the car? Are you on a curving mountain road? Do you feel wind from the open windows, or is the cool air conditioner blowing? Can you feel the hum of the engine, or is it roaring? Smell the fresh interior. What soundtrack are you listening to? Do you have fresh cold lemonade in the cup holder? Take a sip. Enjoy the refreshing taste. Using all your senses paints a clear picture. Visualizing in our mind that which we wish to draw into our life is only the beginning; adding *joy*, our naturally intended emotion, energizes the creative process. Consciously forging our future requires the fuel of *joy* to power the creative mind, like wind to a sail. Imagining a desired event in our mind stirs emotion. By focusing on the joy of this event, we amplify the magnetic power of the universe to draw toward us that which we envision. For example, if we visualize a new family car that we desire, we create a blueprint for the universe. Imagining the joy we will feel when driving this vehicle with our family in the backseat accelerates production. Last, we have to believe. Belief delivers the results. We cannot create anything we cannot believe. This is the biggest challenge for many people. They imagine themselves driving a Ferrari, but do not believe they ever will. If you cannot truly believe you will ever own a Ferrari, I recommend you start with something that fits within your beliefs. Do not sell yourself short, though, by limiting your creation to an old clunker. The act of creating has become a magical experience. To maximize our creative powers, we have to believe.

Believe

I have always had a wild imagination.
Even in my wildest,
Never did I imagine
Life would become more magical
Than imagination could once conceive.
Now, I know that anything is possible
Simply because I believe.

Intent

Along with what we *think*, *say*, and *do*, what we *give* affects what we receive. What we give physically—as well as mentally and spiritually—are returned to us. The Golden Rule exists in most religions and philosophies. "Do unto others as you would have them do unto you" is a simple rule of respect. On a much deeper level, it is a rule of karma, or cause and effect. It is not punishment or reward, it is simply a law of creation; we get what we give.

How we *feel* about giving also affects the result. Our intent drives the experience. It is said that giving is a selfish act, for in giving we shall receive greater than we give. If we are motivated by compassion to help someone, we will be rewarded. If we help someone for our own gain, there is no intent to give. The intent is to receive. Even if we just want accolades, we are still being selfish in our giving. While it makes sense to write off charitable contributions from our taxes, giving just to save money or promote business changes *giving* to *investing*. In 2010, Disney discontinued their offer for free admission on guests' birthdays. Instead, they offered a day at the park in exchange for volunteering to help certain charitable organizations. Receiving free admission to an amusement park for donating time is great; however, it is not really donating if tickets are the motivation—and not the good work itself. Nevertheless, at least the time is being spent helping others, and in the process, perhaps the importance of the work can be stressed. It is often easier to donate money than time; as long as the intent is to give help and not receive personal gain, everyone is better off.

Synchronicity

Being conscious of our intent takes practice. As we practice, we begin to feel guided. Often, this guidance comes from what might be observed as coincidences—little things falling into place at just the right time to lead to a determined outcome. I like to refer to coincidence as synchronicity. For years, I thought I had first learned this concept from the book *The Celestine Prophecy*. The author, James Redfield, does an excellent job of emphasizing the importance of using synchronicity in our lives. While researching the subject, I remembered where I had actually first heard it. In psychology, we studied Carl Jung. The Swiss psychiatrist first published his theory of "acausal connecting principle," or synchronicity, in 1951. His theory refers to coinciding experiences that were thought or dreamed about in advance. Receiving a call from a person you have been thinking about but have not seen in years is an example. It can also refer to a random experience that seems to occur by chance, but also satisfies a need that exists simultaneously. For example, a man was running late to an interview for a sales position. He needed the job, even though the available hours were not ideal for him. On his way, he got lost. Frustrated, he saw a competitor's store and stopped to ask for directions. He saw a sign for a sales position available for the shift he preferred. Instead of going to the original interview, he got hired on the spot. Getting "lost" seemed inconvenient, but it turned out to be a synchronicity. Jung proposed that these events do not occur by chance alone. He believed that all things are connected. If we can be conscious of our connection to our environment, we notice these events more frequently. They are responses from the universe to scenarios we have consciously or subconsciously created in our minds. Our minds relay these messages to our higher self, and it is passed on to the universal network through which all things are connected. Synchronicity is a sign that we are on the right track. This connection between all things that was introduced in psychology has been studied greatly in quantum physics. Physicists are discovering that the separation of objects is illusionary. For example, when photons are separated, no matter how great a distance, a change in one creates a simultaneous change in the other. Science is starting to understand that all things truly are connected on a very deep and very real level. The word synchronicity comes for the root words *syn*, meaning "the same," and *chrono*, meaning "time." Only through a complex set of these synchronicities could I have met my wife.

Skeptics prefer to believe only in chance, while the faithful believe in willful destiny. Circumstances beyond our control combine with decisions we make to lead us through life's cycles. By riding these currents, we find experiences that seem destined for us. Living in the now allows us to seize these moments that seem customized for us, without getting stuck in them. Practicing the balance between "doing" and "allowing" is an ongoing exercise.

Riding the Coincidental Currents

By dark of night
Or bright daylight,
I thrill to harness life's natural motions
And capture its devotions.
I ride the flow of my emotions
To carry me to shore,
Like a tidal wave
That could crush my bones,
Like the joy of love
That mends my wounds.
They call themselves coincidence,
But we know
There is no such thing
As an accidental incidence.

Chapter Eight - **Living in the Now**

The *present* is a *gift* we can live in forever. Living in the now is a crucial aspect of maximizing the human experience. Dr. Wayne W. Dyer, Eckhart Tolle, Louise L. Hay, and many other authors have written extensively on the subject. It is very easy to miss life-enriching opportunities and experiences when we get stuck in the past or while planning or fearing the future. Growth from past experiences is measured by the actions of the present. These same actions determine our future experiences. In moving forward, how do we apply what we have learned to our everyday lives so we may live in the now? What do we *do* with the information to improve ourselves? I believe the method for putting our beliefs into action is a three-step process.

The first step is choice. Understanding that we have free will and are responsible for the outcome of any situation we face empowers us. Whatever the reason for being in our situation, we are the ones responsible to get ourselves out. That does not mean we cannot get help from others; we just cannot expect others to fix our problems for us. We feel much better about helping others who want to do the work to improve their own life. The universe works the same way. God has a way of helping those who help themselves. Being conscious of our everyday choices, we can think, speak, and act in a way that represents the highest light within. This behavior will attract the same in return. More importantly, it will set an example for others to see, as we each have the potential to be beacons of light to others.

The next step is to accept and appreciate exactly who we are at this very moment, not who we were or who we want to be, but the divine existence we are right now. This process of self-discovery is never ending. We are always growing and changing. We also discover different layers within ourselves. We can always learn more of who we are as a parent, a friend, a neighbor, and an individual. The better we know ourselves, the more we are open to improving ourselves. Hiding our weaknesses does not make them go away. Instead, they fester and grow. Facing our issues, we can overcome any personal challenge. Appreciating ourselves as we are keeps us in the moment. Until we do, we cannot move forward with our progress.

The third step is practicing the virtues of love on a highly conscious level in all situations. It is the greatest challenge for me. As great challenges usually are, it is also the most rewarding. Like anything we do, it feels good to see improvement. Feeling calm and relaxed in traffic shows me I have become more patient and tolerant. I do falter, but I do not give up trying. In any situation, we can take a moment to ask, "Does this thought or behavior come from a place of love?" Are we practicing tolerance, compassion, and truth? The practice or act of doing is the ultimate expression of the now. Being conscious of our actions keeps our mind in the present.

Breathing

Staying in the moment can be extremely challenging. We are faced with many distractions. Time passes quickly and must be planned. We have to think about the future. So how do we stay in the present? There are many exercises to help. We do the easiest one all day without a thought. Oxygen is our single-greatest physical need, yet we often take breathing for granted. Focusing on our breath can have many benefits. Taking just one minute to block out everything and concentrate on breathing is a great way to immediately be in the now. Inhaling a full breath for four to five seconds, holding it for two or three seconds, exhaling for four to five seconds, pausing for two seconds, and then repeating this practice two or three times quiets the mind and relaxes the body. This technique is great before taking a test or anytime you want to relax or just be in the moment. Using our breath to relax can be even simpler. Just taking a moment to focus on a few full breaths in and out can give us the mental break and the extra oxygen we need to clear our minds and return to the present. Yoga, Tai Chi, and Qigong are great exercises that incorporate mind, body and spirit. They also teach many valuable lessons and techniques in breathing. Breathing in positive and breathing out negative cleanses and revives. Like the waves in the ocean, the ebb and flow of our own breath sets the rhythm of life.

Personal Choice

It is easy to feel like we do not have choices in life. We limit ourselves by convincing our own minds to believe these self-imposed boundaries. We can unleash ourselves from these limitations only by making the choice to do so. The choices we make determine the opportunities we receive. Life offers us many opportunities to practice living in the now through the personal choices we make. The workplace is one of the best arenas to strengthen our virtues and ethics. Every interaction we have with another person is an opportunity to improve ourselves. Opportunities come from customers, coworkers, and venders. The choices we make throughout our workday make us who we are. When we do what we know is morally right, there is no need to rationalize our choices. Spiritual development in the workplace carries into our personal life as well. Acting to reflect the highest good becomes second nature in all that we do. God is everywhere, including the workplace. I am a part of the company for which I work, just as I am a part of the universal as a whole. I represent both, and they represent me. How can we feel we are separate from any part of life, much less our chosen occupation? Engineering, manufacturing, sales, or service, each offers different challenges and opportunities. The work we do for a living reflects who we are. It does not define who we are. We are that which brings us joy. Once we find what brings us joy; family, art, music, science, or sport, we can *be* that. Until we find a way to make money doing what we enjoy, we can find joy in what we do to make money. Whatever we do, by finding joy in doing it, we find we like it more. In an office, a factory, a classroom, or at home, what we do is temporary. How we do it determines who we choose to be.

Choose a job you love, and you never have to work again.
—Confucius

Although I have been financially successful in sales for a long time, I felt like my career was counterproductive to my spiritual growth. It seemed like a contradiction. Changing my perspective about my field of work, I was able to see the opportunities I could find nowhere else. This career not only gave me the freedom to set my own schedule and potential income, it offered me a chance to prove to myself that I could apply the principles of love; truth, tolerance, and compassion in a world normally perceived as self-serving and egotistical. It was the perfect training ground to achieve my goal of living a spiritual existence in our society.

    I am a writer. It brings me joy. Here I am writing (which I love to do) about the joy I find in what I do for a living. I am a salesman. It is the work I do for income. As with any job, I find pride in doing my job well. Finding joy in what I do makes my job better for me, the company, and our customers. I find joy in my work by seeing it as a field where I am able to practice and exercise my spiritual beliefs in a challenging environment. We all spend much of our lives competing for energy and attention. Sales is a very competitive field, making it a great place to learn about learned human behavior.

    Competition motivates us and others. Motivation follows inspiration. Without motivation, inspiration is just thought. Inspiration is the creative idea. Motivation is the act of following through. Just like a sport, different people have different qualities that make them successful at what they do. When we see our work in perspective with who we are, the *way* we work creates the person we become. Pressure to compete for success can challenge one's ethics. Success can be measured with earthly or spiritual barometers. When we strive for the higher good, we find greater joy on every level of internal and material gain.

    There are people who cheat in many fields; in sports and in sales, too. I have heard many stories of salespeople who cheat in one way or another to get ahead. Instead of working harder or smarter, they take shortcuts or use deception to get ahead. They appear to be more successful by taking advantage of the company that pays them or the customers they are pretending to serve. I once heard about a coworker who openly stated that he would continue to do "whatever it took" to make as much money as he could until he got fired. It is no wonder salespeople have such a notorious reputation. That same individual claimed to be a very religious person. He makes a lot of money and receives a lot of praise for the work he does. He does, indeed, work very hard, but he lacks ethics. His behavior brings in greater income, but less wealth. Cheating wins shallow victories. True wealth is measured in health, happiness, and peace of mind.

Personal Awareness

It is not up to us to judge the success of others. We can leave that to the universe. Our only responsibility is to do what we know is right. That is not always easy. We have been programmed to compare ourselves to others. There are exercises we can do to keep us focused on our own progress. One method is to keep a personal log or journal. I have been recording my experiences, in the form of poetry, since I was thirteen years old. Writing helps me understand my feelings about my different experiences and allows me to organize and express my thoughts. It seems to be a positive way of venting my powerful emotions. Rereading my own words allows me to review my experiences from an outside perspective. I am able to detach myself from my situation so I can offer myself guidance. It is always easier to advise someone in a situation in which we are not involved. When we find ourselves in the same situation, do we follow our own advice?

Advise by Example

All the answers live within us,
But we have been taught
Not to look for answers there.

Without conscious thought,
We search in others
To see our own reflection.

We can see, through them,
The faults in need of correction
To improve ourselves.

Unaware we are looking in a mirror,
It is easy to share invaluable advice
And never know all its worth to us.

Of all we have offered,
How often do we accept and use
All that we have given?

Little advice is worth more
In our own lives
Than that which we give away.

Personal Action

Perhaps you have had similar experiences and feelings as those I am sharing with you. The choices we make determine the opportunities we receive. We are each individually unique, yet we all share the human experience. I want to do what I can to make this world a better place to share the experience. You might want to do so as well. I know of two ways to accomplish this: The first is to learn as much as I can about myself so that I am able to be the best person I can be, and the second is to teach others who they are capable of being by *demonstrating* what I have learned.

When I say "teach," I do not mean "tell." I believe the best way to teach is by doing. Interestingly, it is also the best way to learn. People learn most from practice, second by seeing, and third by hearing. If I see someone's behavior as rewarding, I may choose to replicate it, while I want to avoid behavior with a negative consequence. When words and actions contradict, actions are more believable. Hypocrisy discredits the words of anyone who commits it. It is the greatest obstacle of any person practicing spiritual cultivation in any belief system. Preaching not to judge while condemning others for believing differently is a contradiction. Believing we should treat all people with truth, compassion, and tolerance, why would we strive for anything less?

Teach to Learn

To teach how to
Is not an easy thing to do.

Only through continual learning, as a student,
May one successfully profess.
Through learning, we see how to teach others.
From teaching, we will learn how to reach success.

To do is to teach.
To say is to preach.

When we practice what we preach,
Then we learn and we teach.

There is still much to do,
A lot to teach,
Even more to learn,
And many goals to reach.

Teaching=Doing=Learning=Success

No one can be forced to learn. We can only learn by choice; however, we all teach. Whether we realize it or not, every action we make can be received as a lesson by those around us. For this reason, I strive to be conscious of my behavior so that I might reflect what I have learned. The best way to learn is through practice. Practice is also the best way to teach. Only by doing can we be successful. All the knowledge in the world is useless without action. Doing, not knowing, brings us to our goals. Doing is our goal; therefore, the moment we are doing it, we are successful. If we do nothing, what achievements can be reached?

Idle Man

An idle man is bored and sleeps.
He does not produce.
He cannot gain.
He has to lose.

His purpose and his meaning
Have nearly been destroyed.
Now in their place exists
An ever-growing void.

In 1999, I wrote "Crossing a Millennium," a poem about creating the change and growth we desire by living in the moment. Even after writing it, I still did not realize that I was not following my own advice. I have a habit of being slow to hear what I am saying. The greatest lesson I ever learned on the subject took more than fifteen years. It was writing this book. My goal was to understand my own feelings about the purpose of life on earth. Today I am able to summarize that purpose in one word—*be*. The purpose of life is simply "to be." Just being or existing sounds extremely passive. I desired a more active role. I wanted "to do." We have many different senses with which to experience life. Our senses allow us to observe. Observing is receiving information. Along with receiving, we also transmit information. We do not always have a choice in what we receive, but we always have a choice in what we give. We control our own thoughts, words, and actions. Simply existing in this physical world enriches our spirit. Life has great value in any existence. Being more conscious of our own presence, we can increase the rewards of our human experience. Heightened awareness allows us to actively control our existence. This is "doing." It is an important part of "being." Consciously gathering experience from those you encounter and offering them the highest possible experience in return is deeply fulfilling. Mastering the *art of being* takes conscious thought and effort to keep us in the present moment.

Crossing the Millennia

Counting down the seconds
To see what changes we will find.
Holding our breath in wonder
With great expectations on our minds.

Comparing our achievements
To goals we did not reach.
The passing of a millennium,
What exactly does it teach?

Nothing more, nothing less
Than any point in time.
Only the hype we've built
Makes this moment so divine.

Year after year, new resolutions
Are added to old.
But are these changes really made
As the years unfold?

The crossing of a millennium does not alone
Insure changes to be made,
Nor does the end of a century,
Or the beginning of a new decade.

Growth does not occur over years,
Or months, or even days.
Progress lives in every moment
In which we choose to change our ways.

The evidence can be felt and seen at any time
When we act as we believe.
Living each day as the first of a whole new era,
Imagine the greatness we could all achieve.

Perhaps by living life this way,
Eventually we will see
Every single moment as a starting point
Toward becoming who we want to be.

Amazing as the power of the mind is, change cannot occur in our mind alone. Action determines direction, like the rudder of a ship. We can *think* we want to be healthy all we want. If we do not *act* accordingly with the food we purchase or the activities we chose, we cannot create health. Just as our thoughts require action, our actions require thought. The intent of our actions determines the power of the results.

The question "What would Jesus do?" became very popular in the 1990s. It was even written on bracelets, bumper stickers, and billboards. No one truly knows what He would do. To think we do is awfully presumptuous. Instead, we can ask ourselves, in any circumstance, what is the "right" thing to do? We will know right from wrong. It is important to differentiate between what is right for us and what is right for the higher good. To do this, we have to see if our course of action fits within our understanding of truth, compassion, and tolerance. If we act in accordance to these principles, then we are doing the highest good. Once we train ourselves to behave in this manner, it becomes second nature. Even the smallest issues can be addressed in a way that fits within these beliefs.

Understanding that we have free will, knowing our own strengths, rising to face our challenges, and consciously behaving in a manner motivated by universal love can only make us better people. This is the state of *being* I aim to reach. When we live in this state of mind and spirit, we no longer need to struggle and compete to improve our lives. We can just *be* and feel our lives progress.

"Just *be*" sounds so easy, perhaps it's oversimplified. Life can be very complex. We all have different situations to face. We are in this life together, yet we all choose our own path. This is what I would like to impress most of all. We all learn our *own* lessons. From our own experience, we can offer suggestions and lessons to others. All of us had help getting where we are today. In the end, we are each on our *own* journey.

Let the River Run Through

The flow of life will not be altered
By the hand of man,
But by his soul,
He may pass safely through.

Natural currents
Are fought or ridden,
Like conscious twigs
In the river of life.

Many souls we encounter
Hold firm to the banks,
Afraid of the powerful currents.
Others lie helplessly,
Snagged by the rocks
Beneath their chosen path.
Aware of their own existence,
Lighthearted souls bob smoothly past.

We can extend our paths to others.
We cannot force the change.
As only we can choose our course,
There is no one else to blame.

We are on this ride together.
We get nowhere on our own
Life is a journey.
Our destination is unknown.

Epilogue

Expressing myself through writing, I am able to organize my thoughts and share them without interruption. Unfortunately, the reader is not able to ask questions to better understand my message and opinions. This creates the daunting task of providing enough information to explain my position to those who may not be familiar with a particular subject without belaboring the point to those who are familiar with it.

In high school, my creative writing teacher challenged the class to give detailed descriptions using as few words as possible to fully express an idea. I did my best to accomplish this task. My father warned me that no matter how well I might have done, I would later think of things I wish I had added. I have dealt with that same challenge here. I have explained *my* perspective to the best of my current ability. On some subjects, I may have been redundant, but I would rather overemphasize an idea than not fully express it. I hope, however, that it is "just right" for most. I will appreciate the opportunity to answer any questions I receive to clarify.

I have achieved my goal of organizing my beliefs for myself. If I can help one other person, I will have surpassed my expectations. I am grateful for the opportunity. It has been a great pleasure sharing my experiences. I look forward to sharing more. Perhaps, one day, I will read about yours.

Recommended Reading

Personal experience is the most visceral way to learn, but it is not the only way. There is much to learn from the experience of others. Life is too short to experience all we need to learn firsthand. It is not necessary for any of us to reinvent the wheel. We can take from what others have experienced and add our personal understanding to it. Henry Ford did not event the automobile; he revolutionized its production. Anyone of us can take the knowledge we have gained from others and revolutionize the way that information is used. Rhonda Byrne was not the first to discover the Law of Attraction any more than Christopher Columbus was the first to discover America, although she did bring awareness to a huge number of people who were not familiar with it previously.

I believe most of us have a strong desire to grow spiritually. Studying the great spiritual texts can offer powerful insights for our journey through life. The oldest known spiritual text is the *Tao Te Ching*, which translates to "the book of the virtuous way." It is believed to be over 2,500 years old. As with most ancient scriptures, it has been translated from dead languages through many scribes over many centuries. The most well known translation is eighty-one verses. The book that has been published most is the Holy Bible. It is divided into the Old and New Testaments. The Old Testament and the Torah are the foundation of Judaism. The New Testament is the stories collected by different authors and assembled by Paul over fifty years after Jesus' death. The books of the New Testament are the foundation of modern Christianity, which has fractured into many forms. The Koran is the holy book of the second-largest and fastest-growing religion, Islam. In studying the texts of different religions, we find many repeating themes. In *Parallel Sayings*, Richard Hooper compares the scriptures of the four major religions—Christianity, Islam, Hindu, and Buddhism. He points out similar passages on many different topics. Understanding these similarities encourages unity and tolerance. Modern spirituality also has many of the same themes. I have enjoyed reading the various perspectives on similar topics by many different authors.

I offer you my recommendation of books that have inspired me. The books I enjoyed most rang familiar chords, which felt like they were coming from the core of my being. Some I have read more than once. Many I have passed on. Others have become reference books used on a regular basis. One such book is *You Can Heal Your Life*, by Louise L. Hay, which I mentioned earlier. I believe it is one of the most important books to help begin the process of personal transformation. Another book that seemed strangely familiar from the first time I read it was *The Celestine Prophecy*, by James Redfield. The original nine insights seem like common sense more than revolutionary concepts. His next book, *The Tenth Insight*, is another exciting adventure about the future of our spiritual evolution in the form of a fictional novel. Tom Brown Jr. was the first author to excite me about modern spirituality. His book *The Vision* was the first book I read on the subject. Next I read his book *The Quest*. I enjoyed his autobiographical story of living every boy's dream of growing up under the tutelage of a Native American shaman. Stalking Wolf taught him many lessons about nature. One of his greatest revelations was that the problems of our day can no longer be fixed on a physical level alone. Spiritual change is the only way to save our species. I do believe we are experiencing a spiritual renaissance. An evolutionary shift has begun. I am excited to be a part of this great transformation.

The following are some of the books that have been instrumental in my own spiritual journey:

The Art of Happiness: A Handbook for Living, Dalai Lama and Howard C. Cutler
The Celestine Prophecy, James Redfield
Conversations With God, Neale Donald Walsch
Gratitude: A Way of Life, Louise L. Hay
Gratitude, The Most Powerful Word in the Universe, Trevor Neigebuer
Excuses Begone!, Dr. Wayne W. Dyer
Falun Gong: Principles and Exercises for Perfect Health and Enlightenment, Li Hongzhi
Hands of Light: A Guide to Healing Through the Human Energy Field, Barbara Ann Brennan
Jews, God and History, Max I. Dimont
The Law of Attraction: The Basics of the Teachings of Abraham, Esther and Jerry Hicks
Living Yoga, Georg Feuerstein
One, Richard Bach
Jesus, Buddha, Krishna, and Lao Tzu: Parallel Sayings, Richard Hooper
Parent's Tao Te Ching: Ancient Advice for Modern Parents, William Martin
Practicing the Power of Now: Essential Teachings, Meditations, and Exercises From The Power of Now, Eckhart Tolle
The Quest, Tom Brown Jr.
The Secret, Rhonda Byrne
The Secret of Shambhala: In Search of the Eleventh Insight, James Redfield
The Tao of Pooh, Benjamin Hoff
Tao Te Ching, Lao Tzu
The Teachings, Chief Little Summer and Warm Night Rain
The Tenth Insight: Holding the Vision, James Redfield
To Life: A Celebration of Jewish Being and Thinking, Harold S. Kushner
Touched by the Dragon's Breath: Conversations at Colliding Rivers, Michael Harrison
The Vision, Tom Brown Jr.
The Way of Qigong: The Art and Science of Chinese Energy Healing, Kenneth S. Cohen
You Can Heal Your Life, Louise L. Hay

NOTES

Thank you for reading about my experiences. I invite you to share yours. I would enjoy hearing any comments or questions you may have. I will personally respond to as many inquiries as I can. Please visit my website for more information on how to maximize your own human experience, see a calendar of events, and more.

Markporteous.com

Porteous House Publishing
PO Box 4153
Sanford, Fl 32773
407-549-5021

Or

Mark@markporteous.com